51 WOMEN SENATORS ?

WILL WE EVER HAVE 51 WOMEN SENATORS ? WHEN? HOW WILL THEY REPRESENT US?

WINNIE FROLIK &
BILLY HERZIG

IUNIVERSE, INC.
NEW YORK BLOOMINGTON

51 Women Senators
Will we ever have 51 women Senators? When?
How will they represent us?

iUniverse books may be ordered through booksellers or by contacting:

iUniverse
1663 Liberty Drive
Bloomington, IN 47403
www.iuniverse.com
1-800-Authors (1-800-288-4677)

Because of the dynamic nature of the Internet, any Web addresses or links contained in this book may have changed since publication and may no longer be valid.

ISBN: 978-1-4401-9303-3 (sc)
ISBN: 978-1-4401-9304-0 (ebk)

Printed in the United States of America

iUniverse rev. date: 1/20/2010

This book is dedicated to all the women Senators - past, present and future.

51
WOMEN SENATORS ?

TABLE OF CONTENTS

INTRO

"51 Women Senators ?". That is the title we chose for this book.

51% of the U.S. population is female. For the U.S. Senate to have proportional gender equity would mean 51 women in the Senate chamber. At present there are 17 - a number that is far higher than could have been dreamed not so long ago, but also a testament to how far we still have to go to achieve gender equity in political representation in the United States.

If we take a snapshot of America's racial make up and compare it to a snapshot of the U.S. House of Representatives we see two groups that are under-represented. Hispanics make up 14% of our population and have 25 representatives in the house (5%). African Americans are 13% of our population and have 42 seats in the house (9.5%). Both groups are steadily growing toward more representation.

Then if we look to the Senate we see 1 African American (1%), Roland Burris, from Illinois, who replaced Senator Barack Obama when he was elected President, and 3 Hispanics (3%), Bob Menendez (New Jersey), Ken Salazar (Colorado), and Mel Martinez (Florida).

Election to the Senate has a history of the highest concentration of white male power – more than the House, more than the governorships of the states, and since President Obama's election, even more than the presidency.

Now if we do the same comparison with gender we find that there are 75 women who are members of the House of Representatives (17%), and 17 women in the Senate (17%). If we were to achieve true representative government that is statistically accurate we would have 14 Hispanics and 13 African Americans in the senate…..and we would have **51 women Senators.**

Are we headed for 51? Yes, we think so. As late as 1992 there were only 2 women in the Senate and today's 17 members is an all-time high, so continuing to grow at that rate could get us to 51% somewhere between 2025 and 2040. Remember, men have been running for office and being elected since 1789 and women only since about 1920, but women are catching up.

And how are women doing in the real world outside the Senate? Well, here are some discouraging statistics:

- A year after graduating college women earn just 80% of what men make; ten years down the line they make 69% of what men make.[1] This gap persists even after accounting for such other factors as occupations, parenthood, and the number of hours worked. A typical college educated woman working full time earns $50,000 a year compared to $66,000 a year for the typical college educated man working full time.

- There exists a gender gap in health care; women who call 911 with cardiac complaints are 50% more likely than men to experience delays in getting to the hospital after an ambulance arrives[2]. After they reach the hospital women were 14% less likely to receive aspirin (used to prevent blood clots and prevent repeated heart attacks), 10% less likely to receive beta blockers (which restore regular heart rhythms), 25% less likely to receive reperfusion therapy (used to restore blood flow) and 22% less likely to receive speedy angioplasty to unblock the arteries.[3] All of which goes a long way toward explaining why women are likelier to die than men when they are hospitalized for major heart attacks.

---

1   According to a study conducted by the American Association of University Women

2   Boyles Salynn *Gender Gap in Heart Care Extends to 911* WebMD Health News January 13, 2009

3   Parker Waichman Alonso LLP *Gender Gap in Heart Attack Care* December 9, 2008

- Women make up about 50% of students in law schools but as of 2005, only 17% of the partners at major law firms were women.[4]

- In 2001, women accounted for only 12% of all law enforcement positions in agencies of 100 officers or more. In agencies with fewer than 100 positions, (smaller more rural agencies,) they made up only 8% of all sworn personnel for an average of only 11% of all law enforcement officials being women when women make up over 46% of America's work force.[5]

- A report by the Department of Justice in 2008 showed that rates of domestic violence were 42% higher than had been previously reported and rates of rape and sexual assault were 25% higher.[6]

- A study by Guidestar the national database for non-profit agencies in America found that the median pay for female chief executives at the largest non-profits was $170,180 a year compared to $264,602 a year for their male counterparts; a gap of nearly a hundred thousand dollars! And while women were the chief executives at the majority of non-profit institutions whose annual budgets were $500,000 a year or less, men had 76% of the top positions at organizations whose budgets were $5,000,000 a year or more and 88% of the chief positions at organizations where the budget was $50,000,000 a year or more.[7]

The news isn't all bad of course; girls have caught up to boys in math class[8] and women now make up 48% of undergraduate students

4   O'Brien Timothy *Why do so few women reach the top of big law firms?* The New York Times March 19, 2006

5   **Equality Denied** *The Status of Women in Policing 2001* National Center for Women and Policing

6   *US Soaring Rates of Rape and Violence Against Women* Human Rights Watch, December 18' 2008

7   Lewin, Tamar *Women Profit Less Than Men, in the Non-profit World Too* The New York Times June 2, 2001

8

in math courses at colleges and universities. (As recently as 2005, then Harvard president Lawrence Summers suggested that women were under-represented in math and science departments because of intrinsic gender differences in ability.) Young women have actually began to attend college in greater numbers than young men, (thus fueling worries in conservative circles that the education system is somehow "anti-boy") reform seminaries for future rabbis are now 60% female[9], and Senator Hillary Clinton made 18 million "cracks in the glass ceiling" by running one of the most visible campaigns in American history, proving to be a serious contender, and ultimately becoming Secretary of State. Still, cracks in the glass ceiling are not the same as shattering it once and for all. American women must gain equal political representation in order to become fully equal in society; there is no way around that.

The United States Senate, the upper house of Congress, with only one hundred members has often been described as the most exclusive club on earth. The Senate has the exclusive power in Congress to consent to treaties as a condition of their ratification, to confirm appointments of Cabinet members, military officers, federal judges, and other federal executive positions. The Senate also has the power to consent or confirm impeachment proceedings as well and in the event no candidate received a majority of the electoral votes the Senate would choose the vice-president of the United States.

Senators serve six year terms which leaves them with far more time to concentrate on legislation as opposed to campaigning and there are only two Senators from each state giving each Senator a very large range of constituents to represent. Moreover, the Senate is a notoriously good launching post for an even more exclusive club: the White House. Both candidates for the 2008 presidential election, John McCain and Barack Obama were United States Senators. Hillary Clinton who came closer to the presidency than any other female candidate in history was also a U.S. Senator. As one time Vice Presidential candidate Geraldine Ferraro famously put it: *"When a guy gets elected to the Senate or the Governor's mansion, he wakes up the next morning and says to himself, 'You're presidential material.'"*

9   Fishman and Palmer

Eugene McCarthy declared the U.S. Senate to be "the last primitive place on earth," and Will Rogers suggested we needed an "open day on Senators", but love it or hate it the Senate is the most prestigious, legislative body anyone can be elected to in the United States and that is why when examining the role of gender equity in politics we chose to make the Senate our focus. Also the mathematics are elegantly simple - **51**% women in the population - **51 women Senators**. (By way of contrast 51% of the 435 members of the House of Representatives is 221.85 which is a rather more cumbersome number to deal with.)

This book has five sections:

1) a brief history of women in the Senate so far,
2) a description of the 17 women currently serving in the U.S. Senate,
3) the impact that greater representation of women has in politics,
4) the special challenges that face women candidates, and,
5) speculation: if **51** women were in the Senate - what that would mean for America.

Because women <u>are</u> still playing catch-up and still gaining their equality there are a lot of firsts in these Senators' careers. Whether you agree or disagree with their politics they are amazing and exceptional; inspiring and driven; tough and persistent, with stories of great accomplishments and causes, as well as compromises and defeats.

It would be next to impossible to report every Senator's voting record on every issue, or every accusation. There are many books and biographies, and hundreds of webpages that scrutinize and criticize these women(fairly and unfairly). This book is a starting place to understand the stories of women in the Senate – the past, from the first woman Senator Rebecca Felton, through the present, and into the future toward.... **51**.

"*Tremendous amounts of talent are being lost in our society just because that talent wears a skirt.*" - Shirley Chisholm, the first African American woman in congress

"*There cannot be true democracy unless women are given the opportunity to take responsibility for their own lives.*" - Senator Hillary Clinton

51
Women Senators ?
A Brief History of
Women in the Senate

CHAPTER ONE

"When the women of the country come in and sit with you, though there may be but very few in the next few years, I pledge you that you will get ability, you will get integrity of purpose, you will get exalted patriotism, and you will get unstinted usefulness." - Rebecca Felton the first woman Senator in her address to the House. She held the office of Senator for only one day.

"When people keep telling you that you can't do a thing, you kind of like to try it." - Margaret Chase Smith, Republican Senator from Maine who served from '49 to '73.

Just imagine, until 1993 there wasn't a bathroom in the Senate for women members; they had to use the facilities on the floor below them while their male colleagues were within several feet of a latrine.[10] (If you think this seems a minor ceremonial point, try working somewhere where you are always required to use a bathroom on a different floor for a week or so, and *then* come back to report on the matter.) The lack of a bathroom reflected the attitude of some about women Senators: there

---

10   Foerstel Karen, Biographical Dictionary of Congressional Women Greenwood Press, Westport CT, 1999 pg. 1

weren't many of them and they didn't much matter. And in fact as late as 1992 only two women were serving in the Senate; Nancy Kassebaum, a Republican from Kansas, and Barbara Mikulski, a Democrat, from Maryland. In 1993 four more women were elected to the Senate. While six out of a hundred was still a small minority, nevertheless it was far more women than had ever served at one time.

Still it was not until 1996 that the Senate bothered to honor one of their female alumni by featuring their likeness in the portrait gallery; a painting of Hattie Caraway, the second woman to serve in Congress, the first to be elected to the Senate and the first to chair a Senate committee.

There have been **38 women in the United States Senate** since the establishment of that body in 1789, meaning that out of the 1,897 Americans who have served in the Senate since that time, 1.85 percent of all Senators have been female.

"The day will come when men will recognize woman as his peer, not only at the fireside, but in councils of the nation. Then, and not until then, will there be in perfect comradeship, the ideal union between the sexes that shall result in the highest development of the race." - Susan B. Anthony

To put these statistics into perspective, it's important to remember that the 19th amendment, which granted women the right to vote wasn't passed until 1920. Indeed, many are still alive today who were born at a time when women were not allowed to vote. Despite persistent efforts by women and their male allies it was not until January 12, 1915 that a proposed constitutional amendment to grant women the right to vote was brought up for a vote before the House of Representatives. It lost by a vote of 174 to 204. The proposed amendment was brought before the House again on January 10, 1918 and that year it did pass. Though they could not vote, many women had a keen interest in politics. Surprisingly the famed suffragette and pacifist Jeannette Rankin, the first woman ever elected to Congress, was first elected in 1916 - years *before* the 19th Amendment was ratified! (Though her home state Montana *did* allow women voting rights.)

Thus we had the spectacle of a woman serving in the U.S. Congress who was not legally allowed to vote for herself according to *federal* law. Only 4 days after her term in office began Jeanette Rankin, a lifelong pacifist cast a minority vote against entrance into World War I, which was vilified in the press as a sign of feminine weakness, and ruined her chances for re-election. This followed what was nearly a *century* of agitation on the part of women for the vote beginning with Francis Wright a native of Scotland who emigrated to the U.S. in 1826, and began a series of lectures on the topic. (Some might trace the struggle for suffrage even further to Abigail Adams pleading her husband John Adams to "Remember the Ladies,".)

On the evening before President Woodrow Wilson made a strong and widely published appeal to the House to pass the bill. President Wilson was not always such a strong voice for the rights of women. In his youth, he had in fact once described woman's suffrage as "the foundation of every evil in this country." Later, he took the attitude that woman's suffrage was an issue that should be settled at the state level, with each *state* deciding for itself, questions on who could vote in say, *national* presidential elections. He only announced his support for suffrage, after a group of women calling themselves "Silent Sentinals" (a phrase coined by Harriot Stanton Blatch who first organized the watch in January of 1916) protested in front of the White House holding banners such as "Mr. President—What will you do for Woman suffrage?" "Absolutely nothing," and "Mr. President - How long must we wait for Liberty?." Inez Millholland Boissevain made that plea at a public rally in Los Angeles-and the *moment* the word "Liberty" left her lips she collapsed on the floor. There was considerable speculation as to the cause of her sickness; leukemia, infection, or simply the stress from being on the road constantly agitating for months. What was clear were its deadly results; 10 weeks after the rally Boissevain, known for the contrast between her delicate beauty and Vassar education with her radical suffragist activities, was dead at the age of thirty years old.

Such was the fervor of the times that even a tragedy such as this became fuel for the fiery politics of the time. Boissevain's allies rationalized her death to be the result of the shoestring travel budgets that the movement's speakers were living on, while the *Louisville Times* editorialized *"There are many activities and exigencies in life for which women are better fitted than are men. It is doubtful that political campaigning is one of them. Women have not been at this business long enough to obtain the psychic support which the clamor of the hustings gives the men…The Times deplores any form of activity in politics for the women of either party which is to result in disablement and death.*"[11] (Interestingly enough as we will discuss later, a great many women who gained public office did so because of men prematurely dying during rigorous political campaigns and yet strangely enough, no one has ever speculated as to whether all these unfortunately untimely deaths aren't perhaps evidence that men should stay of out politics…for their own good of course.)

For more than two years over a *thousand* women (mostly upper class women who had the spare time for it) picketed every day and night. When the weather turned cold they had heated bricks from their headquarters across the park transported to them by the janitor in a wheelbarrow to stand on, and thus avoid frostbitten feet.[12] With World War I, going on the Suffragettes even brought in a distinctly flag waving, patriotic war angle to their demonstration.

"Then came the parade, a huge event on Fifth Avenue filled with marched women in blue and gray uniforms, ready to be deployed overseas, or with white on their heads to symbolize bandages and caring for the wounded men. The newspapers said it was not a suffrage parade; it was "a woman's parade." Mothers with the service stars of their fallen sons were in the front, followed by women who had answered the call of their country by filling in for the absent men. There were women census takers, women police, women chauffeurs, "conductorettes and farmerettes," according to news reports. It was an impressive display of the value of women in wartime, and when the votes were counted, suffrage passed in New York with a decisive majority of 140,000 votes."[13]

In January 1918, after years of lobbying and public demonstrations, Wilson finally announced his support of the 19th Amendment guaranteeing women the right to vote. In the meantime the suffragettes were becoming impatient; on February 9, 1919 the protesters burned Wilson's image in effigy at the White House. (Whatever else one thinks of these tactics they certainly proved that lack of political and ideological passion is *hardly* a barrier for women in politics.) The Amendment passed the House but failed in the Senate. At last, on June

11 Clift, Eleanor *Founding Sisters and the Nineteenth Amendment* John Wiley and Sons, Hoboken New Jersey, 2003 pgs. 113-114
12 Clift pg. 127
13 Clift pg. 126

4, 1918, the Senate passed the amendment.[14] It was passed with one less vote than was needed to make the necessary two-thirds majority. The vote was then carried into the Senate. Again President Wilson made an appeal, and on September 30, 1918 the question was put to the vote, but two votes were lacking to make the two-thirds majority. On February 10, 1919 it was again voted upon, and then it was lost by only one vote! There was considerable anxiety among politicians of both parties to have the amendment passed and made effective before the general elections of 1920, so the President called a special session of Congress, and a bill introducing the amendment was brought before the House again. On May 21, 1919 it was passed, 42 votes more than necessary being obtained. Then on June 4, 1919 it was brought before the Senate, and after a long discussion it was passed, with 56 ayes and 25 nays.

It only remained that the necessary number of states should ratify the action of Congress. Within a few days Illinois, Wisconsin & Michigan passed the ratifications. Other states then followed their examples, and Tennessee was the last of the needed 36 states to ratify, in the summer of 1920. Ultimately the deciding vote for Tennessee came down to that of 24 year old delegate Harry Burns, who had previously voted with anti-suffrage forces - had he done so again, the vote would have been tied and there would not have been the 36 states to ratify the Amendment; this time, though, on the pleading of his *mother*, who sent him a telegram saying "Hurrah and vote for suffrage." Harry Burns voted in favor of the suffragettes tipping the vote balance for Tennessee in favor of women's suffrage.[15] As he put it, "I know that a mother's advice is always safest for a boy to follow."

The 19th Amendment to the Constitution was an accomplished fact, and the Presidential election of November 1920, was therefore the first occasion on which women in all of America were allowed to exercise their right of suffrage. The adoption of the 19th Amendment was one of the most important milestones in adapting the U.S. Constitution but as revolutionary moments go it was fairly anti-climactic, (at least initially.)

---

14 Baker, Jean H. *Sisters: The Lives of America's Suffragists.* Hill and Wang, New York, 2005. .

15 Clift pgs. 198-205

"Giving women the right to vote did not have unanticipated consequences like Prohibition. In fact, the shock for suffragists was that it hardly seemed to have any consequences at all. Most women appeared to vote the way their husbands, brothers, and fathers did-not necessarily because they felt obliged to follow the men's lead, but because they shared the same loyalties to class, ethnic group, and region. Like many newly enfranchised groups, women were also voting less frequently than those who had been at it for a long time. In 1920, when women American women went to the polls across the nation for the first time, they made up an estimated one-third of the voters."[16]

In the long term though, the 19th Amendment had changed *everything*. The "gender gap" is one of the most well documented facets of modern U.S. politics that has decided numerous elections from the federal to state level, and women while still not on an equal footing hold approximately 17% of seats in Congress as well 17% of positions in the executive offices of the Fortune 500. It took only two years after the 19th Amendment was passed for a woman to enter the "Senators club," but in that case it was for barely 24 hours!

There is a certain difficulty in writing about Rebecca Latimer Felton, though her historical significance cannot be discounted. She holds not one, not two, but *three* distinctions; she was not only the first woman to ever serve in the Senate, but at the age of 87 years old, she was the oldest freshman senator ever to enter the Senate. Also, she is to this day the only woman Senator from the state of Georgia. She was a strong voice for woman's emancipation and a well respected lecturer in her time. But Rebecca Felton was also a fervent believer in racial segregation who forcefully defended lynching!

It's a rarely spoken but true fact that members of a discriminated group (which Felton as a woman who lived 80 years of adult life in a time when women were denied the vote and could remember a time when women did not even have the right to property within their own name certainly was,) are not themselves inured from prejudices. The fight for women's suffrage began with Lucretia Mott and Elizabeth Cady Stanton, two avid abolitionists being *excluded* from the World Anti-Slavery Convention in 1840 because they were women. This led

---

16 Collins, Gail <u>America's Women; 400 Years of Dolls, Drudges, Helpmates, and Heroines</u> Harper Collins Publishers New York, New York, 2003

seventeen years to the Seneca Falls convention for Women's Rights considered by many to be the foundation of the women's movement in the United States.[17] (One of the featured speakers at that event was the famed former slave autobiographer Frederic Douglass.)

Certainly, rights for women are not, were not, and will never be incompatible with rights for blacks, or vice versa…after all half of African American's *are* women. Jeannette Rankin, the first woman to serve in Congress, was an admirer of Martin Luther King Jr. and organized a protest of the Vietnam War at the U.S. Capitol who among its prominent members present included Coretta Scott King. Rebecca Felton was not of the same stuff as Jeannette Rankin; her views were not merely racist; she actively endorsed what by today's standards are hate crimes. The best that can be said about Rebecca Felton (who had direct memories of Sherman's march to the sea in the Civil War and served as a nurse for Confederate soldiers in that time) was that she was espousing views that were popular among the majority of southern whites at the time, though this in no way excuses her.

Interestingly, and troublingly, Rebecca's notoriety as a defender of Jim Crow was probably a key reason why she was considered appropriate for the temporary position to begin with. So in a cruel irony Senator Felton may have helped break down walls for one historically oppressed group by championing the further oppression of another. In fact, she sometimes championed the cause of women *explicitly* by appealing to racism. As Glenda Elizabeth Gilmore, author of *Gender and Jim Crow* writes, "Felton blamed white men for the grinding poverty in which most rural white women lived. In her attempt to shame them into providing for their families, she declared white farmers to be soft on the rape of white women by black men. Neglectful white men had let things deteriorate to the point that lynching of black rapists was the only remedy, according to Felton. She glorified the antebellum white man, denigrated the postbellum white man, and used the modern black man to goad all concerned." In other words, Felton was trying to make progress for a group that was truly disadvantaged, (poor Southern women in those times did indeed live lives of intense hardship) by making a scapegoat out of the one group of people in the area who had it even worse – black men.

---

17 Clift pgs. 2-15

It would be nice to say that we've evolved far beyond these sort of disgraceful tactics but sadly both the thinly veiled racism coming from certain quarters in our current debates over immigration policy ostensibly in the guise of protecting American workers and the Democratic Presidential nomination process for 2008 have proven otherwise. Senator Obama has been careful to avoid gender stereotypes when campaigning against Senator Clinton; alas she didn't always return the favor. Now Senator Clinton is no Rebecca Felton, nevertheless, many commentators noted that some of her comments only served to pour fuel on what was already an explosive campaign that threatened to create lasting divisions within the Democratic Party. It sometimes appears as if many of the supporters of both candidates were playing the "Oppression Olympics," as blogger Jessica Valenti put it with furious arguments over who had it worse African Americans-or women, in modern society with a healthy side debate over whether it would be more difficult to get a black man or white woman elected President, or in other words was America more racist or sexist? As a writer at the Huffington post pointed out, this might also give you the idea the terms were mutually exclusive and that *African American women* didn't exist at all.

The good news is that there is a long history of support for both women and blacks. In 1851 former slave Sojourner Truth kept the audience at a women's rights convention in Akron, Ohio spellbound with her famous "Ain't I a woman" speech. "The man over there says women need to be helped into carriages and lifted over ditches, and to have the best place everywhere. Nobody ever helps me into carriages, or over puddles, or gives me the best place-and ain't I a woman?"[18] Most younger feminists today, or "third-wave" feminists now choose to examine issues of gender, race, and class as interwoven threads of a broken system and to try to work towards a more equitable system on *all* fronts.

You cannot talk about the history of women in the United States Senate without mentioning Rebecca Felton, the first woman to hold the office of Senator, for however brief a time. To do so would be equivalent to discussing the American Revolution and the formation of the United States without mentioning Thomas Jefferson, (who let

---

18 Clift pg. 25

us not forget, so eloquently championed liberty while owning slaves.) Moreover, her address to the Senate was a call for more women to hold office after her. Yet Rebecca Felton not only held but championed political views that almost all decent people today hold to be repugnant and downright hateful. Should that fact be erased from the record when telling her story? It might make for an easier and more likeable tale of a "gutsy grandma" who helped blaze the trail for women in politics but it would be blatantly dishonest and cowardly to do so much as is the case for those history books who trumpet Thomas Jefferson's rousing words of liberty in the Declaration of Independence but skip over his status as a slave owner. Many men who have made history and paved the way for great things were not only imperfect but in fact had serious dark sides to their life stories. This is no less true for many women who've made history a sign perhaps that the two genders really are truly equal. (Certainly, Senator Clinton amply demonstrated that women are equally capable of brass knuckle campaigning.)

So now finally to Rebecca Felton, the first woman Senator. Born Rebecca Ann Latimer in Decatur, Georgia on June 10, 1835, Felton attended common schools and graduated from Madison Female College in 1852. In 1854 she moved to Bartow County, Georgia and became a school teacher. She married William Harrell Felton, a Methodist minister who shared her interest in agriculture. They also shared an interest in politics; Rebecca served as secretary to her husband while he was a Member of Congress 1875-1881. He also served in the Georgia House of Representatives from 1884 to 1890, and as trustee from the state at large for the University of Georgia from 1886 to 1892. He died on September 24, 1909 at the age of 86, when Rebecca Felton was 64.

In 1922 Governor Thomas Hardwick was a candidate for the next general election to the Senate when Senator Thomas Watson died prematurely. Seeking an appointee who would not be a competitor in the coming special election to fill the vacant seat, and a way to secure the vote of the new women voters alienated by his opposition to the 19th Amendment, Hardwick chose Felton to serve as Senator on October 3, 1922. (Already women voters were becoming a powerful constituency.) Besides being a woman, Felton was well known in Georgia, and at the time of her swearing in she was engaged as a writer and lecturer and resided in Cartersville, Georgia, which she continued until her death in Atlanta, Ga., January 24, 1930.

Felton was well known for her campaigning on the behalf of women and for small farmers; she was also well known (in the tradition of Southern Democrats in her time) for her strict segregationist policies and support of the KKK. On August 11, 1897 she gave a fiery speech proclaiming, "When there is not enough religion in the pulpit to organize a crusade against sin; nor justice in the court house to promptly punish crime; nor manhood enough in the nation to put a sheltering arm about innocence and virtue----if it needs lynching to protect woman's dearest possession from the ravening human beasts----then I say lynch, a thousand times a week if necessary."

When Felton was appointed as Senator, Congress was not expected to reconvene until after the election, so the chances were slim that she would be formally sworn in as Senator. However Walter George won the special election, despite Hardwick's ploy. Rather than take his seat immediately when the Senate reconvened on November 21, 1922, George allowed Felton to be officially sworn in. Felton thus became the first woman seated in the Senate, and served until George took office on November 22, one day later. It was only after Felton's death in 1930 that researchers discovered another speech she had written, in case the Senate *refused* to swear her into office arguing that a women's presence in the Senate no matter how temporary was necessary, *"not as a favor or a compliment, not as a bequest to a charity patient, not as a tribute to personal vanity, but as a tribute to the integrity, the patriotism and the womanhood of blessed wives and mothers of our common country."*[19] When Felton made her entrance on her day in the Senate she was cheered by a large galley of women, she paused in mid-stride to blow her supporters a kiss which made them cheer again. [20]

That Felton was appointed in part because of her husband was until fairly recently not atypical for women in the Senate, (and considering the similar appointment of Jean Carnahan not all that unheard of today either) until fairly recently. Women were allowed the vote but the typical channels of political office which included years and years of politicking and campaigning in their own right before being a serious

19 Foerstel, pg 88
20 Catherine Whitney <u>Nine and Counting; The Women of the Senate</u> Harper Collins, 2001, New York, New York

candidate for the Senate were still barred to them. Before 1992 only six women had attained the *true senatorial* power of being elected to serve at least one full term in office. According to the Center for American Women in Politics, as of today, only 19 of the 38 women who have served in the Senate *initially* entered the Senate through regular elections. (5 others won special elections to unexpired terms while the other 14 were appointed.) Even Hattie Caraway, "Silent Hattie" the first women Senator to be successfully elected into office in her own right owed her initial entrance into the Senate to her husband.

Hattie Caraway's career in the Senate came ten years after Rebecca's famous 24 hours and in that interval no other women served in the Senate. Hattie Caraway was a native of Tennessee, who earned a degree from Dickson Normal College, where she met her husband Thaddeus Caraway. Following the birth of three sons and a move to Arkansas, Thaddeus, after distinguishing himself with a career as a prosecuting attorney on the second judicial circuit, was elected to the U.S. Congress in 1912, as a Democrat and to the U.S. Senate in 1920. Thaddeus served in the U.S. Senate until 1931, when a blood clot in his coronary artery unexpectedly killed him. The question arose of who would serve out the completion of his term. Harvey Parnell, then Governor of Arkansas, decided to appoint Thaddeus's soft-spoken, sincere widow to the post. On December 9, 1931 "Silent Hattie" was appointed to serve out her deceased husband's term in office. A special election on January 12, 1932 saw her victorious, thus making Hattie the first woman to ever be *elected* to the Senate. After she was invited by Vice President Charles Curtis to preside over the Senate she took advantage of the situation to announce that she would run for re-election, much to the shock of many of her male colleagues who assumed she was simply killing time filling her husband's seat. Populist Louisiana politician Huey Long traveled to Arkansas on a 9-day campaign swing to campaign for her.

In 1938 she ran again for re-election against John McClellan and was victorious after receiving support from a successful coalition of veterans, women, and union members. (Senator Caraway like Huey Long was a supporter of many of President FDR's populist policies.) She ran for a final time in 1944 and was defeated by J. William Fulbright. After that, though she continued to serve under President Roosevelt's administration as a member of the United States Employees'

Compensation Commission 1945-1946; member of the Employees' Compensation Appeals Board from July 1946 until her death in Falls Church, Va., December 21, 1950.

In 14 years of service in the Senate Hattie Caraway developed a reputation for two things; her honesty and sincerity, and also, for the fact that she *never* made any speeches on the Senate floor, thus earning her the moniker "Silent Hattie." When openly questioned about this in interviews Senator Caraway responded, **"I haven't the heart to take a minute away from the men. The poor dears love it so."** She was also known to claim that when it came to Senate debate, "We could have much less of it and get more done and save lots of money."

Perhaps Silent Hattie really did just feel that loquaciousness was highly overrated in the Senate; certainly the journal she kept for a time frequently noted her colleagues' tendencies to drone on quite a bit, or perhaps she lacked the confidence to hold the floor. She was in a unique position as the sole women in that august house, who had been put there by her dearly beloved husband's death, and she might well have reasoned, (in all probability correctly), that it was better for her to hold her tongue. In her journals Hattie often displays a more markedly critical, observant, and even drolly witty tongue about the events she was witness to. (Her journal also scrupulously recorded things like candy making with Auntie and luncheons with friends.)[21] And since Hattie did not raise her voice then on the Senate floor, let us take the opportunity to listen to it now, over 75 years later:

December 22, 1931 - "Now they are all discussing Farm Relief as part of the Moratorium. Really seriously, when I know Senator Norris was facetious and sarcastic only in his speech. Just the bad little boy trying to put the other fellow in the hole, when he couldn't have his own way. Senator Morrison was more scared than I'd have been I believe-and so far off the subject-or the grasp of the subject I almost had hysterics especially when I saw the look of awe on Senator Norris' face. And they say women talk all the time. There's been a lot of "old womens' talk" here tonight-but I haven't done any of it."

---

21 Caraway, Hattie Wyatt, Kincaid, Diane <u>Silent Hattie Speaks: The Personal Journal of Senator Hattie Caraway Contributions in Women's Studies</u> Greenwood Press, Westport, CT 1979

January 18, 1932 - "Sen. Lafollette suggested I'd have to get a flashlight to shine enough for the Vice President to see me. I asked him if he were trying to say that was the only way I could shine in the Senate. He disavowed any intention of making such a statement."

February 16, 1932 - "The young LaFollette is fanning the air, and being too dramatic. He is almost persuading me to vote against it. Do wish he would stop. It is his bill, and he's fathering as I mothered my first baby. Everyone must be made to see what a perfect child it is." Hattie did vote for LaFollette's bill in the end despite his grandstanding.

March 14, 1932 - "Today I voted on whether to demand butter for inmates of St. Elizabeth's. I feel that crazy people have as much right to have butter as sane ones, so I voted for butter instead of oleo. Funny. I couldn't feel as if it were of national importance. Maybe I had not thought enough of the cotton seed products. However not being able to grow cotton and make cost of production I feel not so badly. Had luncheon with Sen. Long. He voted with me on this hope it wasn't wrong for that reason. Sen. Logan says he voted aye too because I did-whew-of course my vote counts."

It also becomes clear reading her journal how deeply Senator Caraway felt the responsibilities of her office and the need to carry on Thaddeus Caraway aka "Dad's" work colliding with the expectations for women that she had been raised with. "Every day it is more borne in on my consciousness that to try to fill Dad's shoes is a rather large undertaking. I can but think-I did not try to wear the pants while Dad lived-yet I'm trying to fit my feet into his shoes. I can well know they are easier on my feet than on Parnell's or Kirby's." (Parnell and Kirby were both political rivals to Thaddeus Caraway.) Later, in the spring of 1933 when describing her first meeting with the Attorney General Homer Cummings, "The one thing that broke my heart in that interview was the Attorney General suggested that should my man fail to get the place that I at least am "having the fun of being a Senator." If there is any fun in being a Senator I've yet to find it. My idea of this job is to do my level best to represent the people of my State not only in matters of legislation but in all matters where I can be of service. Enough of this.

These are all things everyone meets face to face in this job, but we are supposed to count it all fun because we are elected to *high* office."

Hattie Caraway did win both her special election and was re-elected into office on her own but her career in the Senate (as did Rebecca Felton's) began with a special appointment as the widows of a prominent man. The third woman elected to the Senate, Dixie Bibb Graves, was not a widow but married to the very much alive Democratic Governor of Alabama Bibb Graves who appointed her to the Senate to (yet again) replace a vacancy brought on by an unexpected death. Dixie Graves is perhaps the most glaring example to be found of a woman whose place in the Senate was due solely because of her identity as a wife.

The first woman elected to the Senate *without* a previous appointment was Gladys Pyle of South Dakota who was also the first woman Senator to serve as a Republican. (25 female Senators have been Democrats while 13 have been Republicans.)

On November 8, 1938 Senator Pyle was elected as a Republican to the U.S. Senate to fill the vacancy caused by the death of Peter Norbeck defeating the Democratic candidate Tom Berry the former Democratic Governor of South Dakota. She served only a couple of short months from November 9, 1938 until January 2, 1939 without even the chance to take the oath of office nor did she seek re-election. Pyle though, (in contrast to Silent Hattie) did appear to get a kick out of the brief time she had on office, driving all the way from South Dakota to Washington D.C. with her mother because, "I wouldn't feel like a Senator unless I did." She also personally screwed her nameplate on the door of her temporary office, organized meetings with Department of the Interior officials to discuss issues relevant to South Dakota, and spoke at a luncheon of the Republican National Committee about the 1940 Presidential Committee exclaiming "This life is a hectic whirl!" After leaving the Senate she remained active in politics and in 1940 became the first woman to deliver a presidential nominating speech for a candidate supporting Harlan Bushfield. She would later serve on the South Dakota State Board of Charities and Corrections for 14 years.[22]

In the history of the Senate 7 of the 35 women to hold office there have taken their seats as a result of the deaths of their husbands, the

---

22 Foerstel pgs 223-224

most recent example is Missouri's Jean Carnahan. Her story is one of a political family and a story of tragedy. Current Missouri Senator Claire McCaskill gets credited as the first woman to be "elected" to the Senate in her state. Jean Carnahan served as Senator from 2001- 2003, so she was Missouri's **first** woman Senator, but she was appointed, not elected. Jean was the state's First Lady when her husband, Mel Carnahan, was Governor from 1993 -2000. They had been married since 1954 and had 4 children. In 2000 Mel was running for the Senate and only a few weeks before the election died in a plane crash along with their son Randy Carnahan. Missouri law does not allow a candidate's name to be removed from the ballot in the last few weeks of an election. The sitting Governor Roger Wilson announced that he would appoint Jean Carnahan if her husband were to win the election posthumously.

Mel's opponent, John Ashcroft (the long-time Missouri Republican who has served as Senator, Governor, and Attorney General), suspended his campaign out of respect for Mel's death and family. Jean accepted Governor Wilson's offer and filmed a campaign commercial. In another Senate first, Mel won the election posthumously and Jean was appointed to the U.S. Senate, but only for 2 years until a special election was held, in which she was defeated by 1% by Republican Jim Talent.

Jean and Mel have two other children who entered politics: Russ Carnahan, a member of the House of Representatives, and Robin Carnahan, who was elected in 2004 as Missouri Secretary of State. Jean has been described as an activist First Lady, working for children's rights and Habitat for Humanity, and was able to participate as Senator for a brief time, and is still writing books as her children now hold public office. Like each of the 7 women Senators who were appointed after their husband's death she has been a contributor to our country through her service, though she took office initially as a replacement under the presumption that she would continue her husband's values.

That 20% of women who have served in the Senate essentially came to it as a "widow's benefit" is quite a striking statistic and has caused some commentary and speculation with many feminists; much as they approve of the idea of greater female representation in Congress and might admire these widows as human beings lament the fact that a woman can't seem to enter office without a husband (or his memory) to push her forward. (Nor is this phenomenon limited to the Senate. The first women Governors Miriam Ferguson of Texas (1925-1927), and Nellie Tayloe Ross of Wyoming (1925-1927), were both wives of former Governors.) Women's Studies Lecturer Martha Ackmann in the *College Street Journal* wrote: "Voters overwhelmingly support the idea of a widow standing in for her husband. A recent Rutgers University study showed that through most of the last century, 84 percent of widows have won their first election. Women seeking office in their own right have won only 14 percent of their initial races. That statistic prompts a disturbing question about gender and politics. Why are voters more likely to elect a woman who stands in, rather than a woman who stands on her own? The answer is clear. The American public still is more comfortable with the idea of a woman acting out her husband's wishes than governing according to her own principles.

Voters elect widows as substitutes for husbands and that is what makes the practice so wrong-headed and—upon deeper consideration— so objectionable. It is not that Jean Carnahan and other widows like her should not hold public office. But to elect a woman at this precise moment only because she is a wife is reductive and demeaning. When widows are tapped to fulfill their husband's terms, voters declare that a woman's marital status is the single most important reason for placing her in office. That attitude reduces a woman to one aspect of her identity—her role as wife—and it reinforces the stereotype that a woman is a mere shadow of her husband: a person who does not function as an autonomous human being."

Ackmann concluded with: "The best way to support women in politics is to encourage women candidates to run for office on their own, addressing issues, and taking their viewpoints to the people. The widow's mandate asks women to enter politics by becoming their husbands—a transformation that is not only impossible, but also contrary to the principles of American equality."

There is certainly a good deal to be said for this reasoning, however, to play devil's advocate the specter of *male* candidates gaining political office through family connections (the Bush family and Kennedy family are only the most prominent examples) it is hardly unknown in America either. While there's a great deal of debate about whether such nepotism ultimately serves the nation's best interests nobody ever claims this practice is demeaning to *men*.

Senator Margaret Chase Smith of Maine, despite being yet another woman whose own political career began with the death of her husband, is considered one of the most successful legislators (male or female) in Maine history. No one would ever argue that as the first woman to win office in *both* houses of Congress, the first woman to set on a U.S. destroyer, and a winner of the Presidential Medal of Freedom her career was anything but distinguished on its own merits. For many years she was known as *the* woman Senator and a somewhat legendary figure. As Catherine Whitney author of <u>Nine and Counting: The Women of the Senate</u> described it, "Margaret Chase Smith was placed on a pedestal along with other female icons-Florence Nightingale, Amelia Earhart, and Eleanor Roosevelt."

Margaret Chase, born December 14, 1897, in Skowhegan, Maine attended in a one room school house, and worked at various jobs with a local paper, a telephone company, and as an executive with a textile mill despite not having a college degree. In 1930 she married Clyde Smith, the then chairman of the State Highway commission. From 1933-1937 Clyde served on the Governor's council. He was elected as a Republican to the 75th and 76th Congresses serving from January 3, 1937 until his death in April of 1940. His widow Margaret filled his vacancy in a special election but instead of living in the shadow of her husband's record she began a political career that eclipsed his in public memory.

During World War II she served on the House Naval Affairs committee, and was co-chair of a sub-committee that investigated problems the War Department experienced establishing bases across the country. Senator Smith played a key role in mediating conflicts between local governments and the military involving the construction of these bases. She served in the U.S. House of Representatives for eight years, but in 1948, she decided to move a step up and run for the Senate seat. She won and was re-elected three more times. In 1960, when she campaigned for a third term, the Democratic party in Maine nominated Lucia Cormier to run against her, making that the first time in Senate history that two women competed for a Senate seat. Senator Smith won that race and kept her seat in the Senate for four terms. She was finally defeated for a fifth term in 1972 after **34 years in office**. She had this to say about leaving office: *"I hate to leave the Senate when there is no indication another qualified woman is coming in. We've built a place here for quality service. If I leave and there's a long lapse, the next woman will have to rebuild entirely."*[23]

Senator Chase Smith's time in office spanned three decades but what was even more impressive was her distinguished service. When first elected in 1948, she received the total greatest vote majority in Maine history. She not only had a record of perfect attendance while in office, but throughout her tenure cast the most consecutive roll call Votes (2,941). She served as the ranking Republican on both the Armed Services Committee and Aeronautical Space Sciences Committee and in 1964 was the first woman to be nominated for the presidency at a major convention. (Barry Goldwater won the nomination and was soundly defeated by Lyndon Johnson in the general elections.) She was the first woman to serve a leadership position in the U.S. Senate, serving as the leader of the Conference of Republican Senators from 1967 until she left office in 1973. She waged a successful campaign for women in the armed services that succeeded in achieving regular status rather than just reserve status for women, and introduced legislation to create the WAVES organization for women who serve or have served in all the sea services including the Navy, Coast Guard, Yeomen F, Marines, and Navy Nurse Corps. (This earned her the nickname "Mother of Waves!")[24] She helped ensure that the landmark Civil Rights Act passed in 1963, included a clause that made it illegal to discriminate against women in hiring, pay, or promotions. (That particular clause, at the time the source for much amusement and ridicule by the press, has in the decades since then helped transform American society.) However, the most defining part of her legacy came in 1950 when, she issued her "Declaration of Conscience," defying Senator Joseph McCarthy.

Like many of her peers, Senator Chase Smith was initially impressed by McCarthy's infamous speech Lincoln Day address blaming American foreign policy failures on infiltration of Communists in the government when he claimed to have a list of known Communists in the State Department. "It looked as if Joe was onto something disturbing and

---

23 Foerstel pgs 254-256
24 Foerstel pg. 255

frightening," she stated and first refused to take issue with him....until she asked "Joe" to provide the proof for his "disturbing and frightening" claims.

A careful examination of the "evidence" McCarthy laid out for her established that his claims were dubious at best and outright fabrications at worst. Senator Chase Smith soon became concerned that McCarthy was fostering a climate of suspicion and paranoia in Washington, particularly among civil servants who were becoming (justifiably as it turned out) terrified that any so-called leftist sympathies could be trumped up into false charges of being that they were Communists. Senator Chase Smith was conflicted about whether to take a stand in the face of McCarthy's growing influence. She was concerned that she had an added sense of vulnerability. Being the only woman in the Senate at the time, she feared she would be dismissed as just a "soft" female. But bolstered by the urging and support of her friends, including the renowned journalist Walter Lippmann, she drafted her "Declaration of Conscience" and sought the signatures of six other liberal Republican senators. (Yes, once upon a time, liberal Republicans *did* exist in politics.) Senator Chase Smith planned to present her statement on June 1, 1950. On her way to the Senate chamber that morning, she encountered McCarthy on the subway line near the Capitol. The following exchange occurred: "Margaret, you look very serious," he said, "are you going to make a speech?"

"Yes, and you will not like it," Smith replied.

"Remember Margaret, I control Wisconsin's twenty-seven convention votes!" he rebutted. Smith took this as an unsubtle threat that he would block her chances of receiving the Republican Vice Presidential nomination in 1952.[25]

Senator Chase Smith's speech, though it lasted only 15 minutes, is one of the most noteworthy addresses ever given in the Senate chamber. Rather than simply provide snippets of this historic moment in courage, we instead present the speech in its entirety...

Mr. President:

---

25 Reprinted from Robert C. Byrd, *The Senate, 1789-1989: Classic Speeches, 1830-1993*. Washington, D.C.: Government Printing Office, 1994. www.senate.gov/artandhistory

I would like to speak briefly and simply about a serious national condition. It is a national feeling of fear and frustration that could result in national suicide and the end of everything that we Americans hold dear. It is a condition that comes from the lack of effective leadership in either the Legislative Branch or the Executive Branch of our Government.

That leadership is so lacking that serious and responsible proposals are being made that national advisory commissions be appointed to provide such critically needed leadership.

I speak as briefly as possible because too much harm has already been done with irresponsible words of bitterness and selfish political opportunism. I speak as briefly as possible because the issue is too great to be obscured by eloquence. I speak simply and briefly in the hope that my words will be taken to heart.

I speak as a Republican. I speak as a woman. I speak as a United States Senator. I speak as an American.

The United States Senate has long enjoyed worldwide respect as the greatest deliberative body in the world. But recently that deliberative character has too often been debased to the level of a forum of hate and character assassination sheltered by the shield of congressional immunity.

It is ironical that we Senators can in debate in the Senate directly or indirectly, by any form of words, impute to any American who is not a Senator any conduct or motive unworthy or unbecoming an American— and without that non-Senator American having any legal redress against us—yet if we say the same thing in the Senate about our colleagues we can be stopped on the grounds of being out of order.

It is strange that we can verbally attack anyone else without restraint and with full protection and yet we hold ourselves above the same type of criticism here on the Senate Floor. Surely the United States Senate is big enough to take self-criticism and self-appraisal. Surely we should be able to take the same kind of character attacks that we "dish out" to outsiders.

I think that it is high time for the United States Senate and its members to do some soul-searching—for us to weigh our consciences—on the manner in which we are performing our duty to the people of America—on the manner in which we are using or abusing our individual powers and privileges.

I think that it is high time that we remembered that we have sworn to uphold and defend the Constitution. I think that it is high time that we remembered that the Constitution, as amended, speaks not only of the freedom of speech but also of trial by jury instead of trial by accusation.

Whether it be a criminal prosecution in court or a character prosecution in the Senate, there is little practical distinction when the life of a person has been ruined.

Those of us who shout the loudest about Americanism in making character assassinations are all too frequently those who, by our own words and acts, ignore some of the basic principles of Americanism:

> *The right to criticize;*
> *The right to hold unpopular beliefs;*
> *The right to protest;*
> *The right of independent thought.*

The exercise of these rights should not cost one single American citizen his reputation or his right to a livelihood nor should he be in danger of losing his reputation or livelihood merely because he happens to know someone who holds unpopular beliefs. Who of us doesn't? Otherwise none of us could call our souls our own. Otherwise thought control would have set in.

The American people are sick and tired of being afraid to speak their minds lest they be politically smeared as "Communists" or "Fascists" by their opponents. Freedom of speech is not what it used to be in America. It has been so abused by some that it is not exercised by others.

The American people are sick and tired of seeing innocent people smeared and guilty people whitewashed. But there have been enough proved cases, such as the Amerasia case, the Hiss case, the Coplon case, the Gold case, to cause the nationwide distrust and strong suspicion that there may be something to the unproved, sensational accusations.

As a Republican, I say to my colleagues on this side of the aisle that the Republican Party faces a challenge today that is not unlike the challenge that it faced back in Lincoln's day. The Republican Party so successfully met that challenge that it emerged from the Civil War as the champion of a united nation—in addition to being a Party that unrelentingly fought loose spending and loose programs.

Today our country is being psychologically divided by the confusion and the suspicions that are bred in the United States Senate to spread like cancerous tentacles of "know nothing, suspect everything" attitudes. Today we have a Democratic Administration that has developed a mania for loose spending and loose programs. History is repeating itself—and the Republican Party again has the opportunity to emerge as the champion of unity and prudence.

The record of the present Democratic Administration has provided us with sufficient campaign issues without the necessity of resorting to political smears. America is rapidly losing its position as leader of the world simply because the Democratic Administration has pitifully failed to provide effective leadership.

The Democratic Administration has completely confused the American people by its daily contradictory grave warnings and optimistic assurances--that show the people that our Democratic Administration has no idea of where it is going.

The Democratic Administration has greatly lost the confidence of the American people by its complacency to the threat of communism here at home and the leak of vital secrets to Russia though key officials of the Democratic Administration. There are enough proved cases to make this point without diluting our criticism with unproved charges.

Surely these are sufficient reasons to make it clear to the American people that it is time for a change and that a Republican victory is necessary to the security of this country.

Surely it is clear that this nation will continue to suffer as long as it is governed by the present ineffective Democratic Administration.

Yet to displace it with a Republican regime embracing a philosophy that lacks political integrity or intellectual honesty would prove equally disastrous to this nation. The nation sorely needs a Republican victory. But I don't want to see the Republican Party ride to political victory on the Four Horsemen of Calumny—Fear, Ignorance, Bigotry, and Smear.

I doubt if the Republican Party could—simply because I don't believe the American people will uphold any political party that puts political exploitation above national interest. Surely we Republicans aren't that desperate for victory.

I don't want to see the Republican Party win that way. While it might be a fleeting victory for the Republican Party, it would be a more lasting defeat for the American people. Surely it would ultimately be suicide for the Republican Party and the two-party system that has protected our American liberties from the dictatorship of a one party system.

As members of the Minority Party, we do not have the primary authority to formulate the policy of our Government. But we do have the responsibility of rendering constructive criticism, of clarifying issues, of allaying fears by acting as responsible citizens.

As a woman, I wonder how the mothers, wives, sisters, and daughters feel about the way in which members of their families have been politically mangled in the Senate debate—and I use the word "debate" advisedly.

As a United States Senator, I am not proud of the way in which the Senate has been made a publicity platform for irresponsible sensationalism. I am not proud of the reckless abandon in which unproved charges have been hurled from the side of the aisle. I am not proud of the obviously staged, undignified countercharges that have been attempted in retaliation from the other side of the aisle.

I don't like the way the Senate has been made a rendezvous for vilification, for selfish political gain at the sacrifice of individual reputations and national unity. I am not proud of the way we smear outsiders from the Floor of the Senate and hide behind the cloak of congressional immunity and still place ourselves beyond criticism on the Floor of the Senate.

As an American, I am shocked at the way Republicans and Democrats alike are playing directly into the Communist design of "confuse, divide, and conquer." As an American, I don't want a Democratic Administration "whitewash" or "cover-up" any more than a want a Republican smear or witch hunt.

As an American, I condemn a Republican "Fascist" just as much I condemn a Democratic "Communist." I condemn a Democrat "Fascist" just as much as I condemn a Republican "Communist." They are equally dangerous to you and me and to our country. As an American, I want to see our nation recapture the strength and unity it once had when we fought the enemy instead of ourselves.

It is with these thoughts that I have drafted what I call a "Declaration of Conscience." I am gratified that Senator Tobey, Senator Aiken, Senator Morse, Senator Ives, Senator Thye, and Senator Hendrickson have concurred in that declaration and have authorized me to announce their concurrence.

Senator Chase Smith expected McCarthy to respond to these strong words, instead he left the chamber immediately following her address. Later he would bestow on her the nickname of "Moscow Maggie," proving once again that insinuations about your opponent's patriotism is the last refuge of scoundrels. He also referred to Margaret Chase Smith and the other six Senators who signed her declaration as "Snow White and the Six Dwarfs," and later on, (in clear violation of Senate customs,) removed her from her position on the Subcommittee on Investigations to give to a new Senator from California…Richard Nixon. A few of Margaret's colleagues in the Senate spoke in favor of her remarks, but mostly they remained silent, intimidated by fears of McCarthy. Senator Smith's mail though, was 8-1 in favor of her remarks and she was congratulated by newspaper editorials across the nation. President Truman personally invited her to lunch saying "Mrs. Smith your Declaration of Conscience was one of the finest things that has happened here in Washington in all my years in the Senate and the White House." In 1954, Senator Chase Smith had the pleasure of voting for McCarthy's formal censure in the Senate and putting an end to his vicious smear campaigns.

And yet…somehow Senator Margaret Chase Smith's historical stand for bravery and integrity has been somewhat obscured. When most academic texts mention Joseph McCarthy they use Joseph Welch who in 1954, famously uttered "Have you no sense of decency, at long last sir? Have you no sense of decency?" as the Great Example of resistance to the infamous Witch Hunt. It doesn't take away from Welch's courage though, to note that Smith's denunciation came four years earlier and, that unlike attorney Welch, she was one of McCarthy's peers. Of course Welch's utterance was easily quotable and memorable…but isn't also "the Four Horsemen of Calumny-fear, ignorance, bigotry, and smear," pretty memorably phrased as well? Is it mere coincidence that Joseph Welch gets mentioned more in the history books? Or is it because when history books are written, men are still considered more suitable in the hero role than women?

Bernard Baruch, presidential advisor to Woodrow Wilson, Franklin Delano Roosevelt, and Harry Truman once said that if Senator Chase Smith's Declaration of Conscience had been made by a man, that man would have been the next President. This is not necessarily a view that Senator Chase Smith (despite her seeking the candidacy at the Republican Presidential election) herself shared. When asked once what she would do if she woke up in the White House, replied, "I'd go straight to Mrs. Truman and apologize. Then I'd go home." Despite the wittiness of her response there is something a little sad in that one of the most remarkable women in United States history and most distinguished persons to ever serve in the Senate didn't dare to imagine herself progressing from the Senate Chamber to 1600 Pennsylvania Avenue.

Margaret Chase Smith was certainly seen as a hero to many young women, and one young woman in particular, a high school senior from Caribou, Maine, one of two youths selected state wide in the United States Senate Youth program funded by the William Randolph Hearst foundation. The student delegates from all over the country toured the monuments, listened to cabinet officials and members of Congress, and could meet with their Senators-if the Senators had time. Much to this young woman's delight Senator Chase Smith, met with her for almost two hours, talking to her and answering her many questions.

"As I left her office with a copy of her speech, I remember being so proud that Margaret Chase Smith was my Senator. I also recall thinking that if she could be a United States Senator, woman could truly do anything."

That high school senior was Susan Collins, the current junior Republican Senator from Maine, who has a signed statement of Senator Smith's creed of public office hanging in her personal Senate office.[26]

*"I didn't want to be one of the boys. I **did** want to be one of the gang."* - Barbara Mikulski.

Perhaps one of the greatest obstacles facing women in the past regarding the Senate is that there were simply no role models or natural mentors for them. Until 1992 there were only two women serving in the U.S. Senate, Barbara Mikulski and Nancy Kassebaum and they were from opposing political parties. No women served from 1922 to 1931, 1945 to 1947, and 1973 to 1978. Since 1978, there has always been at least one woman in the Senate. The Republican Nancy Kassebaum, elected in 1978, while serving in the Senate, was the first woman to serve in the Senate having neither been elected to serve first in the House of Representatives, never having been elected to the political office of a spouse, never having won a special election to win a Senate seat, nor having been appointed to fill out the remainder of a term from a husband after his death while in office or another Senator. She was also the first woman to represent Kansas in the Senate. Prior to

---

26 Whitney pgs. 37-38

that, there were many years where there were no women in the Senate, or only one, woman among a sea of men.

Moreover these women were, whatever their accomplishments, often serving as special appointments to replace a dead spouse. As late as 1992 Senator Barbara Mikulski of Maryland was the *only* Democratic woman Senator to win an election in her own right. This meant that each new woman who came to the Senate was in a sense left trying to find her own way in what was still for all intents and purposes the most exclusive of boy's clubs; something that Senator Mikulski was keenly aware of.

"I was at an initial disadvantage as a woman coming to the Senate, and it wasn't just that the gym was off-limits. I didn't come to politics by the traditional male route, being in a nice law firm or belonging to the right clubs. Like most of the women I've known in politics, I got involved because I saw a community need. And it was tough, absolutely. I didn't have any natural mentors to show me the ropes. I had to seek out my mentors. So when four women finally joined me in the Senate in 1993, I was very gratified. I gladly took on the role of mentor and advisor." - Barbara Mikulski

There is an iconic photo of the Democratic Senate Women in 1993 that prominently features Mosely Braun, Boxer, Feinstein, and Murray-with Barbara Mikulski standing in the exact center in back sporting a huge grin. (All the women in this picture are smiling not just with their lips but with their eyes as well.) It's indicative of the role Mikulski played to the women in the Senate in the adjustment period after their arrival. There is no formal training provided on how to perform the work of a Senator or on the often arcane legislative process of that body. Mikulski as a group did a workshop session laying out everything from how to set up a mailroom, to how to get a incorporation into a bill, to getting good committee assignments. Nor was this something she did only along party lines. When Kay Bailey Hutchison as part of the Republican takeover of the Senate in 1996, came to the Senate, Mikulski issued her an invitation to lunch, on the grounds that, "Civility must start with us." This became a tradition;

each new woman Senator who arrived, Democratic or Republican would get Mikulski's welcoming seminar.[27]

It's worth noting that Mikulski was also at least partially responsible for one of those four new women joining the Senate in 1993. In 1989 Rep. Barbara Boxer began considering moving up from the House of Representatives to the Senate. Boxer had worked with Mikulski before and she decided to seek her advice on the matter. Mikulski urged her-but attached a caveat "If you're ready to leave the House of Representatives and never look back," Mikulski told her, "You can do more here, you can be heard here, and it's worth the fight you'll have to wage to get here. And it will be a fight."

Boxer knew. It was one thing to have been elected to represent 500,000 people. It was another thing to seek election to represent 30 million people. If she decided to run, it would be an uphill battle all the way. Just getting herself that widely known would be difficult. Mikulski gave her diminutive California colleague a reassuring wink. "Of course you could do it for me, Barbara. I need someone around here that I can see eye to eye with."[28]

1992 became tagged the "Year of the Woman" for the unparalleled election of four women to the Senate. In terms of absolute numbers, or percentages four more women is not a whole lot, but when there were only two women in the Senate previously, and never before had so many women been elected to the Senate *simultaneously* in one year, it became a much hyped circumstance among the media; and not entirely to the joy of the women who had been elected. As Senator Mikulski put it, "Calling 1992 the Year of the Woman makes it sound like the Year of the Caribou or the Year of the Asparagus. We're not a fad, fancy, or a year." Senator Mikulski was right about that; while the Senate keeps changing hands, the overall number of women there has been steadily increasing since 1992.

Nor was this phenomenon limited solely to the United States Senate Chamber; by 1994, 4 women were state Governors, 11 women were Lieutenant Governors, 18 of the 100 largest American cities had women Mayors, 1,517 of out of 7,424 State Legislators were women, and 13.5% of them were women of color, and 48 women were

---

27 Whitney pgs. 122-123
28 Whitney pgs. 118-119

members of the United States House of Representatives.[29] The greater representation of women in the Senate was emblematic of a slow but steady revolution across all levels of government; federal, state, and local in the United States where representation of women was growing.

Nevertheless, the media were right to note the historic nature of that year, when a major taboo for women in political office had been broken; in great part as backlash for the perceived mistreatment by the men in the Senate of one woman; Anita Hill. In 1991, millions of American women watched Anita Hill try to maintain a dignified composure in the face of questions about a pubic hair on a can of coke; questions that were posed to her by a group made up entirely of white men. Neither Nancy Kassebaum nor Barbara Mikulski were on the Judiciary Committee though, interestingly the Republican Senator Kassebaum denounced the whole tone of the proceedings stating, "I know it now is expedient for some to attack not only the charges that Professor Hill has leveled against Judge Thomas but to vilify and disparage what has come to be called "this woman." Mr. President, let me make clear that I have no intention of being a party to, quote, "high tech lynching," a phrase I flatly reject as having any validity here, but I also have no intention of being a party to a intellectual witch-hunt against Professor Hill. I see no evidence in the record before us to support any claim that Professor Hill is mentally unstable, is inclined to wild fantasy, or is part of a decade-long conspiracy to get Clarence Thomas. What I do find in this record is much less comforting than these easy and highly speculative theories. What I find instead are serious charges from a creditable witness who has no conclusive evidence to substantiate these allegations, nothing more than that and nothing less." - Senator Nancy Kassebaum at Clarence Thomas' Confirmation Hearing.

This triggered a revolution on several fronts; sexual harassment in the workplace became a national story and lawsuits far more common but it also galvanized woman across the country. Patty Murray of the Washington State Senate had been watching the hearings and seething, wondering "Who's saying what I would say if I was there?" Other women at a neighborhood party reported the same feelings of frustration and anger to her, prompting Patty Murray to make a spur

---

29 Zapatos, Thalia & Kaufman Elizabeth, <u>Woman For a Change: A Grassroots Guide to Activism & Politics</u> Facts on File, NY, NY, 1995 pg. 3

of the moment declaration, "You know what? I'm going to run for the Senate." She not only ran, but won as well as Senators Barbara Boxer and Diane Feinstein, (who were the first Jewish women elected to the U.S. Senate) both California Democrats, (thus making California the first state in America to be represented by *two* women in the Senate) and Carol Mosely Braun of Illinois who was the first (and as of today, last) African American woman elected to the Senate, and the only the woman Senator so far to be elected by the state of Illinois. She was one of only *two* African Americans to serve in the Senate in the 20th century, and was the sole African-American in the Senate from 1993 to 1999. (The Senate's record for representation of people of non-Caucasian ancestry is even *worse* than its record on gender representation; in the entire history of the U.S. Senate there have only been *five* African-American Senators including Senator Obama. This is less surprising though, when you remember that civil rights followed women's suffrage by almost half a century and indeed there are plenty of Americans alive today who vividly remember the days of Jim Crow.)

African-American women are somewhat better represented in the House of Representatives where out of the 87 women serving in the 110th Congress, 12 are African American. Certainly though the facts suggest that the charges that feminism has done less for women of color than for white women are not baseless. This role as a "double minority" Senator must have weighed heavily on Senator Mosely Braun's shoulders. As Judy Woodruff on CNN wrote of Carol Mosely Braun's re-election campaign in 1998, "As the first black woman elected to the U.S. Senate, Moseley-Braun may be 1998's most endangered incumbent. Both symbolically and strategically, hers is a seat Democrats cannot afford to lose."

Senator Mosely Braun certainly did make an impact in her time in office in some respects. She was very liberal on social issues being one of only 16 Senators to vote against the Decency Communications act and only one of 14 Senators to vote against the homophobic Defense of Marriage Act. As she herself described her career, "We've seen the Senate become a different place," she said. "I had to argue about ... and change the Senate around a Confederate flag issue when I first got here. Barbara Boxer held forward on the Packwood issue. Patty Murray has held forward on issues pertaining to children in the classroom. I think all of us have made a difference." It's a sad fact that women of color are often ignored in political surveys and as a result political ideologies and activities among minority women are almost an unknown field compared to the research on white men; and in great part this is because they're simply are not enough of them serving in political office at present. Black women in U.S. politics often have a particularly difficult time of it, balancing expectations of Gender Identity of them with expectations of Racial Identity. Once again, the question of whether blacks or women have it worse is particularly cruel when it ignores the simple fact that plenty of women are black, and half of blacks are women.

This balancing act was made obvious by the controversies weathered by Shirley Chisholm, of New York, the first black woman ever elected to the U.S. Congress, the co-founder of the National Organization for Women (NOW), and first major African American candidate for the President when she made such statements as "I've always met more discrimination being a woman than being black," and "Prejudice against blacks is becoming unacceptable although it will take years to eliminate it. But it is doomed because, slowly, white America is beginning to admit that it exists. Prejudice against women is still acceptable. There is very little understanding yet of the immorality involved in double pay scales and the classification of most of the better jobs as "for men only." This actually brought up accusations that Shirley Chisholm was "betraying" the black community. Whether Congresswoman Chisholm *was* in fact more handicapped by sexism or racism is not for us to say, nor can we say which might prove the greater impediment to successful politicking.

Studies have suggested that people are more willing to *admit* to gender bias than racial bias but that doesn't clear up the issue since *covert* racism can be just as damaging as *open* sexism and possibly even more so. But it's pretty clear that historically speaking, to be both a black person and subject to racism and a woman and thus subject to misogyny at the same time is to really be in a difficult position in political campaigning, (as proof we can look at the fact that while in U.S. History there have been only 25 women Governors including those are currently serving now, not *one* of those women has been a woman of color) which may indeed be why Senator Mosely Braun is still the only black woman to serve in the Senate and only for one term. Senator Mosely Braun herself though when questioned about whether gender or race is a bigger deterrent to gaining political office, stated, "Whether they mitigate favorably or unfavorably frankly depends a lot on the circumstances.

There are some circumstances in which being both black and female is a positive thing. Black women are trained from childhood to be independent and not to look for approval of what we do."

But Senator Mosely Braun was also realistic about the challenges, "Frankly, the downside expresses itself in terms of stereotypes. Women run into the stereotype of being female, weak, and malleable-controlled by men, indecisiveness....Similarly, being black has its own minefield, which again, back to stereotypes, of being lazy, shiftless, criminality, sexuality. So you wind up where you are viewed on one hand as being lazy, shiftless, and oversexed, and on the other hand, where you are earth mother, warm, fuzzy, and people come up to you in public and put their arms around you as opposed to shaking your hand." Senator Mosely Braun declared her candidacy for the Democratic Nomination for President in 2004 as a way of setting an example, she later reported that "What was so exciting about the Presidential campaign was that big burly farmers in the middle of Iowa would come up to me and say, "I think you are right on the issues." New Hampshire was so comfortable. For me, what was edifying was that all that suffering had not been in vain because people were prepared to listen to a candidate who had something to say, who was also female and black." The experience convinced Senator Mosely Braun that the general American public was far ahead of the political class in being open to women or black candidates which is why she was one person *not* surprised by the strength of Senator Clinton or Senator Obama's candidacies, though, she was still well aware that they faced particular disadvantages, because of race and gender, arguing, "But quite frankly, gender is more intractable than race...Gender is much closer to the bone as a social construct."[30]

Senator Mosely Braun suffered from a number of scandals and accusations of doling out favors in office. These controversies certainly

30 Madeline Kunin <u>Pearls Politics & Power: How Woman Can Win and Lead</u> Chelsea Green Publishing Company, White River Junction, VT 2008, pgs. 148-152

tainted her time in office and no doubt contributed to her losing her bid for re-election. Former Senator Mosely Braun always denied all accusations of wrongdoing claiming that she was unfairly targeted due to her visible "double minority" status and the fact that she was widely considered to be extremely far to the left. This perception of Mosely Braun's so-called radical liberalism was not entirely accurate. She was indeed liberal on many social issues from abortion, to discrimination laws, but she could be more conservative on economic issues. For example, she voted in favor of NAFTA and other free-trade agreements. Perhaps the perception of Mosely Braun as a radical leftist was shaped solely on her very liberal social views, or perhaps because in the public eyes of many because people simply *expect* a black woman Democrat to be on the extreme leftward tilt of the party. Neither Senators Clinton or Senator Obama are radicals after all. They are in fact both quite moderate, but they are often depicted as such in the media, perhaps because of race and gender expectations.

Senator Hillary Rodham Clinton of New York has made history for being the first female Senator elected from New York, the first former First Lady to be elected Senator, and, most importantly in the eyes of many, the woman who has come closest to winning the White House. Senator Barbara Mikulski, when giving her endorsement to her colleague Senator Clinton's candidacy for the Democratic Presidential nomination, besides noting Clinton's leadership skills explicitly referred to a desire to break one of the few remaining glass ceilings in government by electing the "first female President." Obviously, a desire to make history by electing the first woman, or the first black man, or the first *black woman* to be the Commander in Chief should not be the only consideration for putting someone into the White House, but there's no denying the psychological allure of helping break down the walls as being a *factor* in the decision process in dealing with a situation where there's more than one acceptable candidate.

A woman as President may still seem far away, but certainly the possibility grows closer each decade, and each year, just as the Senate's inclusion of women has grown from 1 to 17 and continues to grow gradually, toward **51**.

As was mentioned before we cannot give the complete biographies of every woman who has held a seat in the Senate, but here are a few more stories:

Senator Rose McConnell Long was the wife of the famous Huey Long who served Louisiana as Governor and Senator. She became Louisiana's first female Senator when she was appointed after Huey's death in 1935. Rose won a special election in April of '36 to serve the rest of her husband's term but she declined to run for re-election in November '36.

That period of months in 1936 was the first time that two women served simultaneously in the Senate because Hattie Caraway (Arkansas) was also in office. Rose was also the mother of Russell B. Long who served as a Senator of Louisiana from 1948 to 1987.

Senator Maurine Brown Neuberger was the fourth woman elected to the Senate and the first and only woman to serve as Senator of the state of Oregon. She was the wife of Oregon Senator Richard Neuberger. She taught in Oregon public schools and served in Oregon's State House of Representatives.

Maurine won a special election to fill the vacancy of her husband's remaining term after he died of a brain hemorrhage, and she won a general election for the next term January 1961 through January 1967; she did not run for re-election in '66. During her time as Senator she sponsored one of the first bills to require warning labels on cigarette packs and in 1961 President JFK appointed her to be a member of the President's Commission on the Status of Women.

Senator Paula Hawkins (Democrat) is the first and only woman ever elected to the U.S. Senate from the state of Florida. She was the first woman to bring her husband to Washington, D.C. with her which caused the "Senate wives' club" to be known as the "Senate spouses' club". She was defeated for re-election in 1986 by Florida's Governor Bob Graham.

And finally below is a complete list of all **38 women Senators**. We encourage you to research and read each woman's story.

name	state	from	to	party
Rebecca Latimer Felton	Georgia	1922	1922	Democrat

name	state	from	to	party
Hattie Caraway	Arkansas	1931	1945	Democrat
Rose McConnell Long	Louisiana	1935	1937	Democrat
Dixie Bibb Graves	Alabama	1937	1938	Democrat
Gladys Pyle	South Dakota	1938	1939	Republican
Vera Calahan Bushfield	South Dakota	1948	1948	Republican
Margaret Chase Smith	Maine	1949	1973	Republican
Eva Kelly Bowring	Nebraska	1954	1954	Republican
Hazel Hempel Abel	Nebraska	1954	1954	Republican
Maurine Brown Neuberger	Oregon	1960	1967	Democrat
Elaine Edwards	Louisiana	1972	1972	Democrat
Muriel Humphrey	Minnesota	1978	1978	Democrat
Maryon Pittman Allen	Alabama	1978	1978 t	Democrat
Nancy Kassebaum	Kansas	1978	1997	Republican
Paula Hawkins	Florida	1981	1987	Republican
Barbara Mikulski	Maryland	1987	Present	Democrat
Jocelyn Burdick	North Dakota	1992	1992	Democrat
Dianne Feinstein	California	1992	Present	Democrat
Barbara Boxer	California	1993	Present	Democrat
Carol Moseley Braun	Illinois	1993	1999	Democrat
Patty Murray	Washington	1993	Present	Democrat
Kay Bailey Hutchison	Texas	1993	Present	Republican
Olympia Snowe	Maine	1995	Present	Republican
Sheila Frahm	Kansas	1996	1996	Republican
Susan Collins	Maine	1997	Present	Republican

name	state	from	to	party
Mary Landrieu	Louisiana	1997	Present	Democrat
Blanche Lincoln	Arkansas	1999	Present	Democrat
Maria Cantwell	Washington	2001	Present	Democrat
Jean Carnaham	Missouri	2001	2002	Democrat
Hillary Rodham Clinton	New York	2001	2009	Democrat
Debbie Stabenow	Michigan	2001	Present	Democrat
Lisa Murkowski	Alaska	2002	Present	Republican
Elizabeth Dole	North Carolina	2003	2009	Republican
Amy Klobuchar	Minnesota	2007	Present	Democrat
Claire McCaskill	Missouri	2007	Present	Democrat
Jeanne Shaheen	New Hampshire	2009	Present	Democrat
Kay Hagen	North Carolina	2009	Present	Democrat
Kirsten Gillibrand	New York	2009	Present	Democrat

17
CURRENT
WOMEN SENATORS

CHAPTER TWO

Blanche Lincoln, Democrat, Arkansas
Kay Bailey Hutchison, Republican, Texas
Barbara Boxer, Democrat, California
Mary Landrieu, Democrat, Louisiana
Debbie Stabenow, Democrat, Michigan
Susan Collins, Republican, Maine
Barbara Mikulski, Democrat, California
Kay Hagan, Democrat, North Carolina
Amy Klobuchar, Democrat-Farmer-Labor, Minnesota
Patty Murray, Democrat, Washington
Claire McCaskill, Democrat, Missouri
Dianne Feinsten, Democrat, California
Maria Cantwell, Democrat, Washington
Lisa Murkowski, Republican, Alaska
Olympia Snowe, Republican, Maine
Jeanne Shaheen, Democrat, New Hampshire
Kirsten Gillibrand, Democrat, New York

These are the seventeen women currently serving in the U.S. Senate as of 2009. Looking at the list you'll notice only four of these Senators are Republicans and the other thirteen are members of the Democratic party, or in the case of Senator Klobuchar of Minnesota, the member of an affiliate of the Democratic party. According to continuing Gallup Polls, the most recent being from 2009, women voters are more likely to identify themselves as Democrats than Republicans by 41% to 27% (where as men were split 50% - 50%). So it stands to reason that women candidates are more likely to run as Democrats. These poll numbers are directly reflected in the U.S. Senate and the House of Representatives where the men are split by party almost evenly at 50%, but the women Senators and Representatives favor the Democrats by a more than 2 to 1 ratio. The count is always changing each year and sometimes even more often with occasional retirements, changes of party, appointments to cabinet positions, etc. The Senate make up has changed several times in the year spent working on this book.

Currently there are 3 states that now have two women Senators, Washington, California and Maine. Two Republicans, Senator Olympia Snowe and Senator Susan Collins are serving in Maine; perhaps reflecting the lingering legacy of Margaret Chase Smith, while both of California's Senators are Democratic women which might suggest that California (where Harvey Milk became the first openly gay man to win political office) is more progressive, or it might mean that the state that made Arnold Schwarznegger Governor is not particularly conventional in its politics. Both Senators from the state of Washington are also Democrats. The other women in the Senate are spread out geographically from Senator Hagan in North Carolina to Senator Murkowski in Alaska.

Now we'll learn a few facts and highlights about each Senator and how various interest groups and organizations rate their performance. We're not going to tell a complete life story of each Senator but we want to help the reader understand a little about where they came from, where they stand, and where they're going(where they're leading our country).

Senator Barbara Mikulski, Maryland

"The ethnic American is overtaxed and underserved at every level of government. He does not have fancy lawyers or expensive lobbyists getting him tax breaks on his income."

- Senator Barbara Mikulski

Barbara Mikulski of Maryland (Senator Barb) is now in her 4th Senate term making her currently the longest serving woman Senator, 1st elected to the Senate in 1987. She has accepted this role by becoming somewhat of a mentor for women Senators of both parties, to welcome them as they enter the office. Like some of her female counterparts Senator Mikulski wasn't originally planning a career in politics. She received her master's degree in social work from the University of Maryland. So unlike most of the male Senators, Mikulski did not start out as a lawyer but as a social worker for Catholic Charities and Baltimore's Department of Social Service helping at-risk children and helping seniors navigate the Medicaid program.

She first became politically active when she learned of plans to demolish Baltimore's Fells Point neighborhood to make way for a super highway. Senator Mikulski organized the neighborhood communities and put a stop to the highway construction process saving both Fells Point and Baltimore's Inner Harbor in the process. Since Baltimore's Inner Harbor is not only an historic site and iconic landmark but also the city's key tourist attraction, the city owes her a lasting debt for that alone; which took place before she even attained any *official* public office. This helped push Barbara to run for a seat on the Baltimore City Council in 1971. In 1974 she followed that with a run for the Senate but was defeated by Senator Charles Mathias the Republican incumbent; this was the first and last time Barbara Mikulski ever lost an election. In 1976, then Democratic congressman Rep. Sarbanes made a successful run for the Senate and Mikulski was nominated by the Democratic party to take his seat. She won in a landslide and was re-elected four times with little difficulty.

In 1986 she announced her plans for retirement but when the leading Republican candidate for the Senate, Governor Harry Hughes became entangled in the savings and loan scandal, and was replaced by Linda Chavez, Barbara saw a chance to now go for the Senate seat she had lost 12 years earlier; she entered the race and won with over 60% of the vote in spite of (or because of) Chavez's attempts at "gay-baiting" by making insinuations about Senator Mikulski's sexual orientation. (Women, like men, are sometimes not above using sleazy tactics in a campaign.) Barbara has been re-elected by sizable margins in every election since. Mikulski is 72 years old and unmarried. You can Google Senator Mikulski and read pages of speculations and opinions about Barbara's sexual orientation. There has never been an official, on the record question, or answer. Her popularity with male and female voters has been consistent over 30 years.

She is one of only 11 senators to vote against U.S. entry into both the 1991 and 2002 Iraq wars. She endorsed Senator Clinton's run for the presidency citing faith in her leadership abilities and experience and also explicitly voicing an interest in breaking the "glass ceiling" and was in fact the chair of the Hillary Clinton for President Campaign; however, she later publicly endorsed President Obama's candidacy in June and in the convention in August proclaimed "Let's elect Barack Obama and get equal pay for equal work!"[31] Currently Senator Mikulski is Chairwoman of the Retirement and Aging subcommittees and the Commerce, Justice, and Science subcommittee. She is known for taking a strong stance on predatory lending and calling for the investigation of Fairbanks Capital in March 2003 resulting in a major settlement in November of that year.[32]

But Senator Mikulski is not without her critics even among the Democratic party; she voted in favor of the FISA bill granting immunity to telecom companies who cooperated with the illegal wiretapping of American citizens, and was roundly condemned for it by many civil liberties groups who saw this as a capitulation to the worst abuses of the Bush administration. She also voted for the 700 billion dollar bailout of the banking industry in October, 2008 that has now come under a great deal of criticism and scrutiny for failing to provide sufficient oversight as to how the funds would be used.

She has a voting record of 89% according to the Human Rights Council of voting for gay rights, a record of 96% according to the NAACP on voting for pro-affirmative action legislation, a record of 79%

---

31 Democratic National Convention Speeches Archive Tuesday August 26 5:00 pm.

32 "", Office of Senator Barbara Mikulski (2003-11-12)

by the League of Conservation Voters for environmental issues, 90% by the American Retirement Association on senior issues, (perhaps going back to her early career educating the elderly about Medicaid) and has a 100% voting records for Americans United for Separation of Church and State, the ALF-CIO on labor and union issues, by the American Public Health Association on public health policy, by the Campaign for America's Future on Energy independence, by the NEA on pro-public education policy, and by NARAL for reproductive rights.[33] She has a 0% rating from the National Right to Life Committee, Christian Coalition, and the U.S. Border Control lobby seeking to end illegal immigration.

At four foot eleven inches she is tied with California Senator Barbara Boxer for the title of "Shortest Senator".

Senator Blanche Lincoln, Arkansas

"It's not my job to dream your dreams. It's my job to make your dreams become a reality."

- Blanche Lincoln

Senator Blanche Lincoln the senior Democratic Senator of Arkansas was the youngest woman ever to be elected to the Senate when she took office at the age of 38 in 1998; she is now currently the youngest senior Senator in the U.S. Senate and the second female Senator to serve in Arkansas since Hattie Caraway. Unlike Senator Mikulski, Senator Lincoln plunged into a political career from the start; after obtaining her Juris Doctorate from the University of Arkansas she took a position as the staff assistant to Congressman Bill Alexander and served with him until 1984. Senator Lincoln perhaps learned more under her boss than he would have liked; in 1992 she ran against him in the Democratic primary, won, and then went on to win his seat in the House of Representatives where she served until 1997. Being pregnant in 1996 she did not seek re-election. In 1998, after delivering twin boys, she went back into the ring and ran for the Senate seat vacated by the Democratic incumbent Dale Bumpers and defeated her opponent Fay Boozman by ten points.

---

33 On the Issues; Every Leader Political Leader on Every Issue Barbara Mikulski

Senator Lincoln (not surprisingly considering her constituents) concentrates on matters related to farmers and other rural issues. And she sincerely takes an interest in rural and agricultural issues; she's a seventh generation Arkansan, who comes from a farm family and has stated that, "*Some of my favorite childhood memories are of sitting in a duck blind with my father.*" She's one of the key advocates for the Delta Regional Authority that tries to encourage development in the Mississippi Delta Region and is the Chair of Rural Outreach for the Senate Democratic Committee. Senator Lincoln serves on the Senate Finance Committee, Special Committee on Aging, Senate Committee on Energy and Natural Resources, Senate Agriculture, Natural, and Forestry Committee, Senate Social Security Task Force, Rural Health Caucus, and on the New Democrat Coalition. The New Democrat Coalition is a Congressional Member Organization made up of Democrats in the U.S. Congress who describe themselves as "Moderate" and "pro-growth," while other more leftist/liberal members of their party are known to refer to them as DINOs. (Democrats In Name Only.) It was interesting for me to learn that there were "DINO"s and as we will learn later there are also "RINO"s (Yes, Republicans In Name Only).

Senator Lincoln voted for the Iraq war resolution, and was among the minority of Democrats to support CAFTA as part of a record of fiscally conservative voting record on many issues though, with strong support of such social programs as Social Security, SCHIP, and Medicaid. She voted for a ban on partial birth abortion, but voted against parental notification of minors having abortions, and for expanding embryonic stem cell research, and voted to expand hate crimes legislation to include violence motivated by the victim's sexual orientation, and she opposed a constitutional amendment to ban gay marriage.

She has a voting record of 86% with the NAACP and of 89% with the HRC demonstrating a record of pro-gay rights and pro-affirmative action votes. Her record with the ACLU is 60% for a mixed record on civil liberties votes and a record of 50% with NARAL for a mixed record on reproductive rights but has the endorsement of EMILY's List of pro-choice women. She has a record of 78% with the Chamber of Commerce demonstrating her pro-business stance and a low rating of

32% with the League of Conservation voters showing a pattern of anti-environmental votes, and a rating of 58% with CATO Center Institute for Trade Policy showing a mixed record on trade issues as well as a mixed record of 50% on public health issues, but has a strong record 77% with the ALF-CIO on union issues and 70% rating with the ARA on Senior issues. She has a 91% voting record with the NEA on education issues and only 16% rating with the Christian Coalition, an 8% rating from the U.S Border Control demonstrating her "open border" stance and 0% rating from the National Life to Right Council.

Senator Kay Bailey Hutchison, Texas

"I have long believed that taxpayers make better use of their money than the government ever could."

- Kay Bailey Hutchison

Senator Kay Bailey Hutchison, senior Republican Senator from Texas, is a lot of firsts. She was the first woman to represent Texas in the U.S. Senate, the first Republican woman to win election to the Senate against an incumbent candidate, one of the first on-screen newswomen in Texas, and she became the first U.S. Senate candidate to poll more than 4 million votes in 2000. She is currently the most senior Republican woman in the Senate ranking 35th out of a' 100 and in 2001 she was ranked one of the 30 most powerful women in America by *Ladies Home Journal.* She is a true conservative, and a true Texan. Kay's Texas roots run deep. Her great, great grandfather, Charles Taylor, was one of the signers of the Texas Declaration of Independence in 1836.

Senator Hutchison was a cheerleader in college and a member of the Pi Beta Thi Sorority at the University of Texas. She received her J.D. from the University of Texas Law school (which did not accept former President George W. Bush) in 1967. After graduation she became the political and legal correspondent for the Houston channel KPRC-TV. Her public notoriety helped her win election to the Texas House of Representatives in 1972 where she served until 1976 and then was Vice-Chairwoman of National Transportation Safety Board from 1976-1978. She ran for the United States House of Representatives in 1982 but lost whereupon she temporarily retired from politics and became a bank executive and successful businesswoman.

She returned to politics in 1990 when she ran for and was elected as the Texas State Treasurer and in 1993 won a special election held to fill the Senate seat vacated by Lloyd Bentsen, who had resigned to become Secretary of the Treasury under President Clinton. She won re-election in 1994, 2000, 2006 all three times by a landslide despite being indicted in 1993 on charges of official misconduct and records tampering. The prosecution though, was not able to present any evidence at the time of her trial so Hutchison was acquitted immediately.

In 1993 Senator Hutchison showed her empathy for American women by sponsoring the "Homemaker's IRA" that passed in 1996; this legislation increased the sum that homemakers were allowed to put away in tax-free Individual Retirement Accounts from $250 a year to $2500 raising their IRA savings limits to match that of their working spouses. She also joined women of both parties to support and pass legislation to give rape victims the same protections as victims of other crimes. So, even though a strong conservative Republican her record shows she is more likely to occasionally "cross over" on political issues than either her former colleague Texas Senator Phil Gramm or his successor Senator John Cornyn. She is also one of the few Texas Republicans in either house of Congress who is pro-Choice.

Texas is an oil state and Senator Hutchison has received more campaign contributions from large oil and gas corporations than any other member of the Senate, and she supports oil drilling in the Arctic National Wildlife Refuge. In 2005 she sought to curtail the rights of plaintiffs to file class action suits against major corporations. Senator Hutchison serves on the Senate Appropriations Committee, Veterans Affairs Committee, Committee on Rules and Administration, and Committee on Commerce, Science, and Transportation.

Senator Hutchison has a 0% rating from the HRC on gay rights, a 0% rating from the ARA on senior issues, a 0% rating from the AFI-CLO on union issues, a 0% rating from the APHA on public health issues, a 5% rating from the LCV on environmental issues, an 18% rating by the NAACP on affirmative action, and 25% by the ACLU on civil rights. (Senator Hutchison is the living embodiment that not all women politicians are progressive on social issues.) Her rating of

36% by the NEA indicates her mixed record on public education. She has a 100% rating by COC showing her adamantly pro-business views and 67% by CATO for her endorsement of free trade. She also enjoys a 100% rating with the Christian Coalition and 75% with the USBC showing her support for measures against illegal immigration.

She was mentioned as a running mate for Senator McCain in 2008, but when interviewed by George Stephanopulous on ABC TV's "This Week" stated, "Senator McCain has a lot of options...I don't want to be vice president." But there is growing talk and interest in her possibly making a run for Governor of Texas.

Senator Diane Feinstein, California

"Winning may not be everything but losing has little to recommend it."

- Diane Feinstein

Senior Senator of California Diane Feinstein holds the distinction of being first in several areas of California and American political history. She was the first female President of the San Francisco Board of Supervisors, the first female Mayor of San Francisco, the first women to serve in the Senate from California, is one of only two Jewish women in the Senate, (the other is Barbara Boxer also from California) the first woman to serve on the Senate Judiciary Committee, and the first woman chair of the Senate Rules committee and Senate Intelligence Committee. She also happens to be ranked the fifth wealthiest Senator according to CNN.[34]

A 1955 Stanford graduate, Feinstein was appointed by Governor Pat Brown to serve on the California Women Parole Board in 1961. In 1969 she was elected to the San Francisco Board of Supervisors where she was elected president. She served there for nine years until November 27, 1978 when Dan White assassinated San Francisco Mayor George Moscone and Supervisor Harvey Milk. Diane Feinstein as president of the Board of Supervisors made the announcement to the press and was automatically appointed to the post of Mayor. In 1979, she was elected in her own right, and was re-elected in 1983.

---

34 Loughlin, Sean; Robert Yoon (2003-06-13). "", CNN

As mayor she helped secure federal funding to rebuild San Francisco's cable car system. She oversaw planning to erect high rise buildings in San Francisco and in 1987 *City and State* magazine named her America's Most Effective Mayor, and during the '80s she also served on the Trilateral Commission. She wasn't free of controversy however; in an infamous press conference on Richard Ramirez she revealed confidential details that investigators believed impeded their pursuit.

In 1990 she ran for Governor of California and lost to then Republican Senator Pete Wilson. In 1992 she was fined for failure to disclose campaign contributions. Ironically enough the Senate seat Pete Wilson gave up to assume the office of Governor was won by Diane Feinstein in a special election in 1992 making her the first woman Senator to be elected in California. At this same time another Californian in her 5th term in the house of reps, Barbara Boxer was elected for the other Senate seat which was open with the retirement of longtime favorite Alan Cranston. So the 2 women were actually elected to the 2 California Senate spots the same day. Since Feinstein was elected to an unexpired term she took office a few months sooner than Boxer and thus is known as the "senior" Senator. She has since been re-elected in 1994, 2000, and 2006.

In 2001 she won the Woodrow Wilson award for public service. Although Feinstein has been sometimes labeled a liberal, she has also at times weighed in as more of a moderate in support of some traditionally conservative issues such as the death penalty. She not only voted for the Iraq war resolution in 2002 but for emergency funding of the war in 2007, something for which she has been roundly criticized by members of her own party and for her support of further government surveillance, wiretapping, and general erosion of civil liberties to fight the war on terror. She was the Democratic co-sponsor of the USA PATRIOT Act and one of only six Democratic Senators to approve Michael Mukasey's appointment as Attorney General. She is often referred to as a pro-business Democrat and at times as a DINO (Democrat In Name Only). She is a pro-Israel member of the Council on Foreign Relations and is also a member of the American Israel Public Affairs Committee. On gun control and environmental issues she has been more typically aligned with her party.

As a super-delegate, Feinstein originally backed Hillary Clinton for the Democratic presidential nomination; months later after Senator Barack Obama won the nomination she shifted her support to him. Because she believed in both candidates and the importance of party unity Feinstein suggested a private, one on one meeting between Clinton and Obama and arranged the use of her Washington, DC home for the meeting. [35]

Feinstein's marriage to investment banker Richard Blum has led to scrutiny of some of her votes on foreign trade issues because of her husband's business dealings with China. There have been accusations of "conflicts of interest" suggesting that Feinstein's votes may have benefited some of the companies that Blum owns. All accusations were denied by Feinstein and she has provided financial disclosures to distinguish her holdings from her husband's.

Senator Feinstein has a 100% rating from NARAL on reproductive rights. She has a rating of 88% with HRC on gay rights and of 89% with the NAACP on affirmative action but only 60% with the ACLU on civil liberties. The LCV gives her 79% on environmental issues and CAF gives her a 100% for energy independence. AFL-CIO also gives her 92% on union issues while the COC only gives her 39% for pro-business legislation while CATO gives her 45% on Free Trade. APHA gives her 88% on public health while NEA gives her 91% for pro public education, and 70% from ARA on seniors issues. USBC gives her only 7% on curbing illegal immigration and her rating with the Christian Coalition is 0%.

Senator Barbara Boxer, California

"Really life is complicated enough without having a bunch of Senators decide what we should do in the privacy of our own homes."

- Barbara Boxer

Barbara Boxer, currently the junior Senator of California, holds the record for the most popular votes in a contested statewide election in California, having received nearly seven million votes in her re-election victory in 2004 against Republican challenger Bill Jones. Preferring the

---

35 ", CNN (2008-06-08)

term "progressive" over "liberal" through her years in the House and the Senate Boxer has tended to be a little further to the left than her fellow California Senator Diane Feinstein, although the two women are close on many issues.

Boxer's views towards war have been consistent over time, protesting the Vietnam War in the '70s, voting against the Gulf War in the '90s as a member of the house and voting against the Iraq War Resolution as a Senator in 2002, which she has publicly claimed to be the *"best vote of my life"*.

She has been responsible for some memorable quotes; be they notable gaffes such as "*Those who survived the San Francisco earthquake said 'Thank god I'm still alive' But of course those who died their lives will never be the same.*" ....or truly stirring moments on rhetorical eloquence, "*For the sake of troops, for the love of troops, we must not add yet another casualty to this war. We must not let truth be a casualty of this war.*" An inspiring public speaker, Senator Boxer at 4'11 shares the title of "Shortest Senator" with Barbara Mikulski of Maryland, and in fact has a box known as the "boxer box" to stand on at public speaking events to raise her to the height of the podium.

The headline-making Senator Boxer was born in New York where she graduated from Brooklyn College with a degree in economics and worked as a stockbroker while her husband Stewart attended law school. The couple moved to California in in late '60s. In 1972 she had her first political campaign running for the Marin County Board of Supervisors. She lost. She later worked as a journalist for the Pacific Sun and as an aide of then Congressman John Burton.

In 1976 she ran again for the Marin County Board of Supervisors and won. She served for six years and became the first woman president of the board. In 1982 she ran for the U.S House of Representative under the slogan "Barbara Boxer Gives a Damn." (That slogan sums up the tone of Boxer's unique and pugnacious political style.) She won and was re-elected five times.

In 1992 she was one of hundreds of Representatives who let their checking accounts become overdrawn known as the "House Banking Scandal". These congressmen and women did not break any laws, and the checks didn't bounce because, the House Bank provided overdraft protection, but it was none the less a public embarrassment that so many of these public servants and supposed leaders were unaware of what they were spending. Boxer publicly apologized for not paying enough attention to her account and wrote a $15 dollar check to the Deficit Reduction Fund for each of her 87 overdrafts.

During her time in Congress, Boxer served as a member of the House Armed Services Committee and exposed the Pentagon's use of $7,600 coffee pot. In 1991 she led a group of women House members to the Senate Judiciary Committee *demanding* that the all white all male Committee of Senators take Anita Hill's charges seriously. This helped propel 1992's "Year of the Woman" and Boxer's own successful candidacy to the Senate. She won her first Senate election in 1992 by three points, her second Senate election in 1998 by ten points, and her third. As a Senator she has authored, co-authored, and/or sponsored many bills and acts including the Patient's Bill of Rights in 1997, the Violence Against Women Act and the Violence Against Children Act. In 2004 she co-authored the Invest in the USA Act with Republican Senator John Ensign from Nevada, which makes possible the creation of 600,000 American jobs and gives American companies incentives to bring profits back from overseas. And in 2005 Boxer added an amendment to the Foreign Affairs Reauthorization Bill that requests that the government of Saudi Arabia permit their women vote in elections and run for office.

The administration of George W. Bush was met by much opposition from Boxer. While most of the 16 women Senators disagreed with President Bush on a few issues(older Republicans Elizabeth Dole and Kay Bailey Hutchison siding with Bush most often), Boxer was an outspoken non-supporter. She voted against Bush's nomination of John Bolton to the seat of U.S. Ambassador to the U.N., against John Roberts as nominee for Chief Supreme Court Justice, against Samuel Alito as Supreme Court Justice, against Alberto Gonzales for Attorney General, and against Condoleezza Rice as Secretary of State. She was also one of only 2 Senators to be in favor of a Democratic resolution to censure George W. Bush proposed by the Senator from Wisconsin Russ Feingold. (The other vote in favor of the censure came from Senator Tom Harkin of Iowa.)

She established the Excellence in Education award to recognize teachers, parents, businesses, and other organizations working to make positive changes in education. She successfully led the 2003 Senate floor battle to block oil drilling in the Arctic National Wildlife Refuge. She co-sponsored the Violence Against Women Act and Title X Family Planning Services Act. She voted against the Iraq war in 2002 and in 2005 co-sponsored a Senate Resolution calling for a time table for US troops to withdraw from Iraq. She has also been an outspoken proponent for women's rights overseas, "*It is in Saudi Arabia's best interests to allow women to fully participate in its society, and this includes the right to vote and run for office.*" and for sanctions against perpetrators of crimes against humanity in Darfur.

She has a 100% rating from NARAL on reproductive rights, HRC on gay rights, NAACP on affirmative action issues, CAF on energy independence, APHA on public health, AFL-CIO on union issues, and AU on separation of church and state issues. The LCV gives her an 89% on environmental issues, the NEA 91% on pro-public education votes, and ARA gives her 90% on senior votes. The ACLU gives her 60% a mixed record for civil liberties and COC gives her 22% on business issues, and 17% from CATO since Boxer promotes "fair-trade" rather than "free-trade." Her 9% from USBC shows Senator Boxer's open border stance and both the National Right to Life Campaign and Christian Coalition give her a 0% rating.

Boxer is also the author of several novels in which her main character is a liberal woman Senator.

Senator Mary Landrieu, Louisiana

"*A penny saved is not a penny earned if at the end of the day you still owe a quarter.*"

- Mary Landrieu

Senator Mary Landrieu, the senior Democratic Senator of Louisiana, comes from a politically active family; her father Maurice Edwin "Moon" Landrieu was the former Mayor of New Orleans and her brother Mitch Landrieu is the current Lieutenant Governor of Louisiana. After graduating from Louisiana State University in 1977 Mary went to work as a real estate agent for the next two years. In 1980 she was elected to the Louisiana House of Representatives and served there until 1988 when she became the Louisiana State Treasurer where she served until 1996. In 1995, she ran for governor but came in third during the primary.

In 1996 she was elected to the U.S. Senate in a very close and hotly contested race. She prevailed with less than six thousand votes making it the narrowest margin of victory for a Senate race that year. Her opponent demanded an investigation claiming electoral fraud which the Senate Rules Committee agreed to investigate. A month into the investigation though, it turned out that the detective, Landrieu's opponent Karl Jenkins had hired to investigate the alleged fraud was paying off witnesses to make false claims of electoral fraud. The detective also had numerous felony charges on his record including a guilty plea of attempted murder. The Democrats resigned from the probe in disgust but the investigation continued for 10 months with the end result that the elections original results stood and Senator Landrieu's status was formally legitimized.

Senator Landrieu is (as often the case with Democrats from below the Mason-Dixie line) one of the more conservative Democrats in Congress and considers herself a Blue Dog Democrat while others less charitably have called her a DINO (Democrat in Name Only). She voted for the confirmation of Supreme Court Justice John Roberts, (though she opposed Samuel L. Alito) and supports drilling in the Arctic National Wildlife Refuge. Landrieu supports eliminating the estate tax permanently, and voted for the Bush tax cut passed in 2001. In 2005 she was one of only four Democrats to vote against repealing the portions of the tax cuts passed in 2001 and 2003 that more liberal Democrats have charged unfairly benefit the wealthy.

Hurricane Katrina destroyed Landrieu's lakeside New Orleans home, and hometown. The Senator has become a national spokeswoman for victims of the hurricane and has complained of "the staggering incompetence of the national government." In a TV interview with Chris Wallace, Landrieu called the evacuation of New Orleans prior to Hurricane Katrina "the best evacuation." She also commented that "most Mayors in this country have a hard time getting their people to work on a sunny day." She co-sponsored the Hurricane Katrina Disaster Relief program earmarking $250 billion to rebuild the city.[36]

---

36 Stolberg, Sheryl Gay (September 9, 2005). "". .

On February 26, 2009 she called for the resignation of Doug Whitmer FEMA chief of staff of the Louisiana Transitional Recovery Office in New Orleans after an investigation by CBS news detailed cronyism, sexual harassment, and racism in his office.

"Yesterday, I was hoping President Bush would come away from his tour of the regional devastation triggered by Hurricane Katrina with a new understanding for the magnitude of the suffering and for the abject failures of the current Federal Emergency Management Agency. Touring this critical site yesterday with the President, I saw what I believed to be a real and significant effort to get a handle on a major cause of this catastrophe. Flying over this critical spot again this morning, less than 24 hours later, it became apparent that yesterday we witnessed a hastily prepared stage set for a Presidential photo opportunity; and the desperately needed resources we saw were this morning reduced to a single, lonely piece of equipment. The good and decent people of southeast Louisiana and the Gulf Coast -- black and white, rich and poor, young and old -- deserve far better from their national government. Mr. President, I'm imploring you once again to get a cabinet-level official stood up as soon as possible to get this entire operation moving forward region-wide with all the resources -- military and otherwise -- necessary to relieve the unmitigated suffering and economic damage that is unfolding."

- Mary, during 1st days of Hurricane Katrina

Senator Landrieu is on Emily's List of pro-choice women candidates thought her voting record with NARAL is a mixed 43%. She's rated by the ACLU on civil liberties, 89% by the HRC on gay rights, 86% by the NAACP on Affirmative Action. Her 78% rating with the COC and 77% rating with the AFL-CIO put her in the rather unusual position of having both a strong pro-business voting record and strong pro-union voting record with a rating of 42% by CATO for a mixed rating on trade issues. She enjoys a 91% rating with the NEA on pro-public education but only 50% from the APHA on public health, and 50% by the ARA on Senior issues. CAF only gives her 33% for energy independence and a low rating of 21% by the LCV for environmental issues. USBC gives her 33% rating showing a more open policy toward immigration issues and the Christian Coalition gives her only a 16% approval rating on her votes.

Senator Deborah Stabenow, Michigan

"We have come a long way. There is a long way to go, but I think the decisions are better made as women are participating."

- Debbie Stabenow

Of the 80 plus male Senators there are none with the background of being a social worker. Of the 17 women Senators there are 3. Junior Senator Deborah Stabenow of Michigan won her first election when she was still in grad school. While earning a master's degree in Social Work from Michigan State University, (graduating *Magna Cum Laude,*) she successfully ran for the Ingham County Board of Commissioners where she served from 1975-1978 while continuing to do work as a social worker and leadership training consultant being inspired to do so by threats to close a local nursing home. (Just as Senator Murray's career began over threat of closing a daycare center and Senator Mikulski first started organizing because bulldozers threatened the neighborhood.)

From 1979 to 1990 she served in the Michigan State House of Representatives and became the first woman to preside over the House. While in the Michigan Senate she passed numerous property tax cuts, authored a domestic violence law requiring stronger penalties on persons who committed domestic violence, and was a leader in passing educational reforms and legislation to protect families and children. She then went on to serve in the Michigan Senate from 1991-1994. In 1994 she launched an unsuccessful primary run for the Michigan Governor's office and was then selected as nominee Congressman Howard Wolpe's running mate but they lost to the incumbent candidates.

In 1996 she was elected to the U.S. House of Representatives and was re-elected in 1998. In 2000 she did not seek re-elected to the House of Representatives but set her sights on the Senate and squeaked by with a narrow victory. This made Senator Stabenow not only the first women Senator from Michigan but also only the second person from Michigan to win election to both houses of Michigan's State Legislator as well as the U.S. Congress. In 2004 she became the third ranking Democrat in the U.S. Senate as Secretary of the Democratic Caucus. In November, 2006, after winning re-election with fifteen points, she left her caucus secretary position to become the Chair of the Democratic Steering and Outreach Committee, succeeding Senator Hillary Clinton.

While in the senate, Senator Stabenow authored the first law to ban drilling in the Great Lakes, helped broker an agreement in 2006 for the Canadian province of Ontario to stop dumping its waste in Michigan within the next four years, and was a leader to stop the privatization of Social Security saying, "*Social Security is not just the foundation of America's retirement, dignity, and security, it ensures the economic stability and strength of our families and our state's economy.*" Not surprisingly for a legislator from Michigan Debbie Stabenow has been a very vocal voice for labor issues and the importance of preserving manufacturing jobs in the United States. Stabenow also led in the passage of the one of the first laws in the U.S. that required all Michigan children to ride in car seats until age 5 and she authored a law which increased criminal penalties for those who commit domestic violence.

Senator Stabenow has a 100% voting record with NARAL on reproductive rights, and with the NAACP on affirmative action, the NEA on pro-public education, CAF on energy dependence, the APHA on public health, and the AU on separation of church and state. She has an 89% voting record with the HRC on gay rights 90% with the ARA on seniors issues, 85% with the AFL-CIO on union issues, and 85% with the LCV on environmental issues. Her record with the ACLU on civil liberties is more mixed at 60% and she is rated in at 39% with the COC on pro-business legislation. CATO gives her only 17% record on "free-trade" voting, Stabenow being a proponent of "fair-trade." Her open border stance is reflected in her record of only 25% with the USBC and the Christian Coalition gives her a voting record of 0%.

Senator Olympia Snowe, Maine

"In today's world, it is no longer unimaginable to think that business can operate - and even thrive - in an environmentally-friendly manner."
- Olympia Snowe

Maine's Senior Senator Olympia Snow was named one of America's Top Ten Senators by Time Magazine in 2006.[37] She was the only woman on the list. She enjoys one of the highest approval ratings in the Senate in her home state and is considered the most liberal/moderate

---

37 ", Time (2006-04-14)

Republican in Congress. Snowe earned an B.A. in political science from the University of Maine in 1969. Soon after she entered politics and was quickly elected to the Board of Voter Registration, working for then Congressman William Cohen. When her husband Republican Maine State Legislator Peter Snowe was killed in a car accident in 1973, Olympia at the urging of friends and colleagues ran for his vacant seat. She was 26 years old at this time.

She was re-elected in 1974 and in 1976 she was elected to the Maine State Senate. Then in '78 she was elected to the U.S. Congress where she served from 1979 to 1995 on the Budget Committee and International Relations Committee. During her time as a Representative she developed a relationship with another young Representative form Maine, John McKernan, who was to become Governor of Maine. When the 2 were later married Snowe was the state's 1st lady for 3 years while still holding her seat in the House of Representatives, making her the 1st woman to be a member of Congress and a 1st lady of a state simultaneously.

In 1994 she won her current Senate seat by over twenty points. Along with her fellow Senator from Maine, Susan Collins, she voted against impeachment of President Clinton. When she was re-elected in 2000 she won by over thirty points; in 2006 she was re-elected to a third term with 74% of the vote, the second largest margin of victory for any U.S. Senate in the country. (Senator Richard Lugar of Indiana who had the very largest victory margin didn't even have a Democratic opponent to run against.)

Snowe is the fourth woman to serve on the Senate Armed Forced Committee and the first to chair its seapower committee that overseas the Navy and Marine Corps. In 2001 she became the first Republican woman to get a seat on the Senate Finance Committee. She has never lost an election, she was the youngest Republican woman ever elected to Congress, and the first woman to serve in both branches of the state congress and then both branches of the U.S. congress. She is the 1st Greek-American woman to serve in Congress and is a member of the Greek Orthodox Church. She helped pass a genetic non-discrimination act. She is generally fiscally conservative but opposed NAFTA and CAFTA. On taxes Snowe voted against the Bush tax cuts along with only a few Republicans(one of who was Senator John McCain who campaigned as president in '08 supporting the idea of such tax cuts).

She supported McCain in his presidential run and was thought to be a good choice as McCain's VP running mate because of her 30 years experience and high level of popularity....but remember, she is known as a moderate and the choice of the pro-life conservative Governor Sarah Palin for the vp spot was an attempt to solidify interest in the right side of the Republican party. It is notable that all of the Republican, female Senators had more experience than Governor Palin and that Palin's relative lack of experience pales in comparison to Snowe's, or for that matter to Alaskan moderate Republican Senator Lisa Murkowski.

NARAL gives her a rating of 83% on abortion rights, HRC 78% for pro-gay rights, while the NAACP gives her 57% for a mixed voting record on affirmative action programs. The ACLU gives her 60% for civil liberties. COC gives her 65% for pro-business legislation while CATO gives her 58% for free trade legislation and AFL-CIO gives her 31% for being generally unfavorable to union policies. Her 25% rating from the USBC indicates an open borders position on Immigration. She has a mixed record of 55% from the NEA on public education and 38% for public health issues according to APHA and a very low 10% from ARA on seniors issues. CAF gives her a rating of 67% on energy independence while the LCV gives her 74% on environmental issues. The Christian Coalition gives her voting record only 50%.

Senator Susan Collins, Maine

"Taking the time to read to children is not only a worthwhile investment but also a wonderful experience. I have visited 119 schools in Maine, and these visits are among the most rewarding experiences in my career of public service."

- Susan Collins

Susan Collins is the junior Senator from Maine, working with senior Senator Olympia Snowe. Like Snowe, Collins is also a Republican, also moderate, and also pro-choice. She has been a strong supporter of stem cell research which is the opposite viewpoint of most members of her party. She has a strong family history in public service; both her father and mother served as Mayor in her hometown Caribou. Family roots run deep, five generations of the Collins family have been involved in Maine's lumber industry.

Senator Collins graduated Phi Beta Kappa from St. Lawrence University. From 1975 until 1987 she worked for Maine Senator William Cohen. Another point in common of Olympia Snowe and Susan Collins is that they each spent time working for Cohen. Snowe worked for Representative Cohen in the early '70s and later succeeded him to represent Maine's 2nd district in the House when Cohen moved on to the the Senate. Collins worked for Cohen while he was in the House and also when he became Senator and ultimately succeeded him in the Senate when he took the job of Defense Secretary in '97. In between her years working for Cohen and her 1996 run for senate she had an unsuccessful attempt to run for Governor in '92.

In 1996 she won her first race for the Senate by five points, in 2002 she won re-election by over fifteen points, and in 2008 was re-elected again by over twenty points. Senator Collins is known for being a political moderate so much so that she has sometimes been called a RINO (Republican in Name Only). She (along with fellow Republican Senator Olympia Snowe) voted to acquit President Clinton during his impeachment trial and she was the only Republican to be endorsed by HRC in 2008. She's also known for being pro-choice.

She voted with the Iraq war resolution and the Kyl-Lieberman agreement authorizing President Bush to use military force against Iran, and she voted for the confirmation of Supreme Court Justices Samuel L. Alito and John Roberts.

In 2003 she was the only Republican to vote for limiting a tax cut in order to help certain rural hospitals and in 2005 she sponsored a bill for mental health service for older Americans. Collins was the coauthor of the Collins-Lieberman Intelligence Reform and Terrorism Prevention Act of 2004(With Connecticut Senator Joe Lieberman)which put in to effect certain recommendations of the 9-11 Commission to update and modernize American intelligence. Then in 2005 Collins and Washington Senator Patty Murray co-authored legislation to strengthen U.S. port security which was signed by president Bush. Collins went the opposite way as her fellow senator Snowe by supporting the Bush tax cuts(Snowe voted against).

She has an 83% voting record with NARAL for Reproductive Rights, and 78% with the HRC on gay rights. Her record on affirmative action, public education, and civil liberties is more mixed with a 40% rating by the ACLU, 55% with the NEA, and 57% with the NAACP. She has a 67% rating with CAF on energy independence and 68% with the LCV on environmental legislation. She has a lower rating with the APHA of 38% on public health and 0% with the AFL-CIO on union issues and with the ARA on senior issues. She has a 25% rating with the USBC indicating a more open borders policy on immigration issues while a rating of 78% with the COC shows her strong pro-business leanings as her 67% rating with CATO demonstrates her free trade stance, (though, she did vote against CAFTA.) The Christian Coalition gives her a 66% voting record with them. (Does that translate into a one in three chance of going to hell?)

She was one of six Republicans to be endorsed by the Human Rights council in 2008, and one of only three Republican lawmakers to vote for President Obama's stimulus package known as the American Recovery and Reinvestment Act. She has also been a strong supporter of stem cell research. Senator Collins cannot be confused with a liberal Democrat but she has shown herself to be far more willing to cross party lines on key legislation than most of her fellow Republicans in the Senate. She truly appears to mean it when she proclaims, *"We will have to work together in a bi-partisan spirit and with our international partners if we are going to achieve progress and peace now and for future generations."*

Senator Elizabeth Dole, North Carolina

"The last century was known as the "American Century." In a single lifetime, I have seen Americans split the atom, abolish Jim Crow, eliminate the scourge of polio, win the Cold War, plant our flag on the surface of the moon, map the human genetic code and belatedly recognize the talents of women, minorities, the disabled and others once relegated to the shadows. We are now in the earliest years of a new century ... writing another chapter in American history."

- Elizabeth Dole

When the idea of this book began long-time Republican Elizabeth Dole, Senator from North Carolina was still in office. She was defeated only recently(November '08), so we'd like to include a brief profile of her. Dole's journey includes 30 plus years of government service before running for the Senate. Her resume is long and impressive having worked in the administrations of four Presidents.

Born in North Carolina she is a graduate of Duke University and Harvard Law School. Early in Dole's career she identified herself as a Democrat and campaigned for Kennedy and Johnson, and later worked in the White House for President Johnson's administration. When Richard Nixon was elected President in '69 Dole worked for him in the Department of Consumer Affairs, then from '73 to '79 with the FTC(Federal Trade Commission). She became a Republican in '75 and married Republican Senator of Kansas Bob Dole. She participated in her husband's '76 VP campaign as well as his 1980 unsuccessful run for President.

A series of high-profile positions followed in the '80s and '90s giving Dole opportunities to serve in leadership roles when two more Republican Presidents appointed her to Cabinet seats. President Ronald Reagan appointed Elizabeth U.S. Secretary of Transportation and George H. W. Bush made her Secretary of Labor.

Then in '91 she became president of the American Red Cross, a job she took without payment. She resigned in '99 to pursue a bid for the 2000 Republican Presidential Nomination. Although she dropped out early in the race, before the primaries, she was well-received by the public and her party and her name was in the running for Vice-President on the George W. Bush ticket, a spot that ultimately went to VP Dick Cheney.

When she decided in 2001 to run for the North Carolina Senate seat that was becoming available with the retirement of Republican Jesse Helms she would bring to the table all her years of experience in various campaigns and positions. She won that Senate seat in 2002 with 54% of the vote. During her term she was a member of the Committee on Armed Forces, Committee on Banking, Housing & Urban Development, the Committee on Aging, and the Committee on Small Business & Entrepreneurship.

There was an ongoing question about Dole's residency. She moved her residency back to North Carolina in 2001 after not living there since 1959, and has also kept her main residence in DC with her husband since 1975. State law require that if a Senator or Representative has an out of state residence then they should be planning to return to North Carolina and make it their primary place of residence at some point.

Elizabeth Dole's career has been that of a diplomat, a spokesperson, an appointee- in contrast to the background of grassroots social activism of Senators such as Barbara Mikulski of Maryland, and Patty Murray of Washington state. Thus, her approaches to problem-solving have been more likely to work within the system. Her style has been to use her skills as a communicator, and an administrator, and she has been described as someone who can hold a seat or title and carry out the challenges of that role, rather than a crusader.

After a long, distinguished career in politics her run as Senator came to an end after only one term as she was defeated in the 2008 election by North Carolina native Democrat Kay Hagen. Hagen's woman for woman victory in the election keeps the female Senator count from declining.

Senator Kay Hagan, North Carolina

"This state needs a work horse not a show horse. I want to be that work horse."

- Kay Hagan in her campaign against Senator Elizabeth Dole

Junior Senator of North Carolina Kay Hagan was elected in 2008 after having defeated the incumbent Senator Elizabeth Dole, the first time one woman candidate defeated another incumbent woman candidate in a Senate race and also making North Carolina the first state to have elected female Senators from two different parties. Senator Hagan's father and brother both served in the Navy and her father was elected Mayor of her childhood hometown Lakewood, Florida. Hagan earned her J.D. from Wake Forest University and entered private practice with North Carolina National Bank (now known as Bank of America) eventually becoming vice president of estates and trusts. After having her first child, though, she resigned to become a stay at home mother. She did, though, find the time to be a local manager for the gubernatorial runs of Governor Jim Hunt. (As niece to the now deceased Florida Governor Lawton Chiles, who never lost an election, this was a world she was quite familiar with.)

In 1998 she ended up working on her own election campaign to the North Carolina General Assembly as a state Senator. Given that Senator Hagan has not had time to develop a voting record in the U.S. Senate it seems better to look to her record in North Carolina where she served five terms. In her service for the state Senate she became known as a pro-business Democrat. She was chairwoman of the body's Appropriation's Committee and Pensions, Retirement, and Aging Committee. Hagan was known for her pro-education policies supporting legislation raising teacher's salaries and increasing funding for early childhood education. Her victory over Senator Dole was the widest margin of victory for North Carolina in a Senate race in over thirty years; possibly fueled by public anger over Senator Dole's use of a negative campaign ad calling Senator Hagan "Godless."

Senator Hagan now serves on the Committee on Armed Services and Committee on Health, Education, Labor, and Pensions. The former committee assignment must have deep personal significance to Senator Hagan; her attorney husband is a Vietnam veteran, her father in law is a two star general in the Marine Corps, and she has one nephew in the Air Force and another nephew who's a Navy Seal. Notably, even before the current housing crisis Senator Hagan when in the state Senate passed legislation mandating that "Personal Financial Literacy" be taught to North Carolina's high school students. It is still early in Hagen's U.S. Senate career so we can't say how each interest group and organization will "rate" her, but by coming this far in politics surely she has learned that you can't please everyone. So let us wish her well and hope for the best.

Senator Amy Klobuchar, Minnesota

"In my job you can't just put your head in the sand and throw partisan bomb shells. You have to get results."

- Amy Klobuchar

Senator Amy Klobuchar, of the Minnesota Democratic Farmer Labor Party(DFL), is the first woman to be elected to the Senate from the state of Minnesota. The DFL is a major party in Minnesota created in 1944 by the merging of the Minnesota Democrats with the Farmer-Labor Party by Hubert Humphrey(U.S. Senator from Minnesota and 38th Vice President during the term of President LBJ.) Amy is the first "elected" woman of Minnesota because there was another woman who previously served in the U.S. Senate from Minnesota. Muriel Humphrey, the widow of Hubert Humphrey was appointed to his Senate seat in 1978 following her husband's death, making her the first wife of a Vice President to hold public office. Muriel served the remainder of the term from January to November of '78.

At this writing it is still to be determined whether Klobuchar will be the junior or senior Senator because it is also yet to be determined who the winner is/was in the 2008 Minnesota Senatorial election. (Should newbie Al Franken win Klobuchar would be the senior and if Norm Coleman regains his previous seat he will also regain his seniority, making Klobuchar the junior.)

While Senator Klobuchar is one of the youngest Senators she has an impressive resume and list of accomplishments (from high school valedictorian to U.S. Senator). She has been cited by The *New York Times* as one of the seventeen most likely women to become the first female President of the United States.[38] She received her bachelor's degree *magna cum laude* in political science from Yale University while participating in the Yale Democrats and Feminist Caucus. Her senior thesis *Uncovering the Dome* a 150 page history on the politics surrounding the Hubert H. Humphrey Metrodome in Minneapolis is now a widely used college textbook. She received her J.D. from the University of Chicago Law School and was associate editor of the Law Review. In 1998 she won election as the Hennepin County attorney making her the chief prosecutor for the most highly populated region of the state of Minnesota. She ran for re-election in 2002 and was unopposed. She was *Minnesota Lawyer's* 2001 Attorney of the Year. She also managed to be partner in the highly prominent global firm of Dorsey and Whitney while serving as a prosecutor. From November

---

38 Zernike, Kate (2008-05-18). "", *New York Times*

2002, to November 2003, she was president of the Minnesota County Attorney's Association.

In 2006 she enjoyed a landslide victory of over twenty points against her Republican opponent in the Senate race that was the largest U.S. Senate election margin in the state of Minnesota since 1978. As of 2006 she has been serving on the Senate Agricultural Committee, Senate Environment and Public Works Committee, Senate Commerce Committee, and the Congressional Joint Economic Committee. She voted for the "Protect America Act" but against legal immunity to telecom companies that illegally participated in wiretapping. She is pro-choice, supports LGBT rights, favors social services like Social Security and universal health care, and has been a public critic of the Iraq war. Less than a week after the collapse of the I-35W Mississippi bridge, Senator Klobuchar introduced and succeeded in passing emergency legislation to appropriate $250 million to quickly build a replacement bridge. She voted in favor of banning the use of waterboarding.

In March 2007, Klobuchar went on an official trip to Iraq with colleagues Sen. Sheldon Whitehouse (D-RI), Sen. John Sununu (R-NH) and Sen. Lisa Murkowski (R-AK). Klobuchar returned with a pessimistic note for the Iraqi cabinet. She noted that U.S. troops were completing their job and working arduously to train the Iraqis, but voiced her frustration with Prime Minister Nouri Al-Maliki.

Having served only a few years of her first 6 year term Senator Klobuchar hasn't had as much time to accumulate scores and ratings as some of the other longer-serving Senators but: She received a grade of A+ from the Iraq and Afghanistan Veterans. She received a 100% rating from NARAL on reproductive rights, and a score of 0 by the Christian Coalition. The NAACP rated her at 97%, and the ACLU at 57% in 2007. Representing a farming state she received a high score of 91% approval from the Farmers Union. Klobuchar was also rated very highly on both pro-business and environmental issues, sometimes a tough line to walk.

She supported Barack Obama in '08 in his presidential campaign. At the April '09 announcement of the retirement of Supreme Court Justice David Souter, Senator Klobuchar was mentioned as a possible nomination for the slot.

Senator Patty Murray, Washington

"Guess what - I am one of the ONLY senators in the whole United States Senate who is computer literate!"

- Patty Murray

Because of the age of most Senators and the fact that they have helpful staffs, that opening quote is probably pretty accurate. Senior Washington Senator Patty Murray from the state of Washington is also the only known member of Congress to use the description "a mom in tennis shoes" as the catch phrase of her campaign. Senator Murray received her B.A. from Washington State University and then went on to teach pre-school children for a few years. Few Senators(men or women) come from a background of teaching. From 1984 to 1987 she taught at Shoreline Community College and became a parent volunteer for the Shoreline Community Cooperative School a parent-child education program sponsored by the very community college where she was working.

A political career she always stated was the last thing on her mind at the time but one day she heard a teacher announce that the school would be closing because the Washington State legislature had rescinded their funding. Patty Murray went to Olympia Washington to talk with state legislators and convince them to restore the funding. As the story goes she finally got an interview with one legislator who informed her, "Lady that's a really nice story but you can't get the funding restored. You can't make a difference. You're just a mom in tennis shoes."[39] Murray was ticked off by this; she was so ticked off in fact that she put together a list of 15,000 parents and showed up at every hearing; within a year the program was reinstated and her political career had begun. She used that phrase "mom in tennis shoes" successfully in her campaign for the Shoreline School District Board of Directors (1985-1989), Washington State Senate (1989-1993), and finally in her run for the U.S. Senate, in 1993 when then Democratic incumbent Brock Adams was accused of sexually assaulting multiple women. When she 1st ran for a seat in the Washington state senate in 1988 she said, *"I'm running because I have young kids. We need policy makers who understand what women are going through so these policies work for women"*.

---

39 Kunin pg. 27

Here's another quote from Patty later on as a Senator: *"Public education is the bedrock of our democracy. It helps create good, active citizens, and it gives our families the tools they need to put food on the table and a roof over their heads. It also ensures that each generation of Americans will have more opportunities than their parents and grandparents did."*

She is only the fourth Washington Senator to win three consecutive terms. She was chairwoman of the Democratic Senatorial Campaign Committee from 2001-2003 and is currently the Senate Major Conference Secretary the fifth highest rank in the U.S. Senate. She is a senior member of the United States Senate Committee on Appropriations and the chairwoman of its Transportation, Housing, and Urban Development, Related Agencies Subcommittee.

Senator Murray is the daughter of a purple heart awarded disabled veteran of World War II and is proudly the first woman to serve on Senate Veteran's Affairs Committee. She was one of the 21 Democratic Senators to vote against the Iraq war resolution in 2002.

She also serves on the Committee on Health, Education, Labor and Pensions, Committee on the Budget, Committee on Rules and Administration, and the Joint Committee on Printing. In January 2008, she endorsed Hillary Clinton's campaign for the presidency despite Washington's votes in ballots going almost 70% for Barack Obama.[40] After Clinton's concession she gave her endorsement to Barack Obama. Senator Murray co-sponsored legislation to create the Wild Sky Wilderness area in the Washington Cascade mountains region, the first federally designated Wilderness area in Washington, state, since 1984 and offers protection to significant amounts of low elevation, high productivity forest. She has also been a major opponent of plans by the US Air Force to use the French corporation Airbus to build refueling tankers rather than Boeing which is based in the state of Washington; and employs 50,000 of Senator Murray's constituents.

She has a 100% voting record on reproductive rights according to NARAL, pro-gay rights according to HRC, pro-public education rights according to the NEA, on public health according to the APHA, on separation of church and state according to the AU, and on energy independence according to CAF. The LCV gives her a 95% rating on environmental issues, the NAACP 93% for affirmative action issues,

---

40   Hillary for President 2008 1-30

the ARA 90% on seniors issues, and AFL-CIO gives her an 85% on union and labor issues. CATO gives her a rating of 42% on free trade issues, and the COC 43% on pro-business votes. The USBC gives her a rating of 0% on anti-illegal immigration efforts, (Senator Murray is a vocal supporter of open borders,) and the Christian Coalition gives a big fat 0% rating.

Senator Maria Cantwell, Washington

"It's time for a change, and it's not an issue of being old. It's an issue of longevity."

\- Maria Cantwell

The third state with an all-women line-up in the Senate is Washington. In 1993 as Patty Murray was elected to the Senate, Maria Cantwell was elected to the House of Representatives where she was the 1st Democrat to be representing Washington's 1st district since '53, briefly breaking 40 years of Republican rule. Maria was born in Indiana where her father was a county commissioner and state legislator. She was the 1st member of her family to graduate college when she got her degree in public administration from Miami University in Ohio. She then relocated to Seattle to work on the campaign of Democratic presidential contender Alan Cranston who had served for over 20 years as a Senator from California. Maria led a successful campaign to build a new public library in the suburbs of Seattle. In 1986, at the age of 28, she was elected to the Washington State House of Representatives where she helped write the Growth Management Act of 1990, regulating cities development and then helped it pass. She also worked on legislation regarding nursing homes and retirement facilities. Then in '92 she was elected to the House of Representatives but served only one 2 year term and was defeated in her attempt for re-election in '94 by Republican Rick White in the mid term rush that gave Republicans majorities in both the House and the Senate.

She was defeated in part because of her support for NAFTA and then President Clinton's budget plan. For the next six years, she stayed out of politics working in marketing for the Internet media delivery service known as RealNetworks based out of Seattle. Thanks to stock options in the company she became a millionaire. In 2000 she sank ten million into her Senate campaign, pledging not to use PAC money, a pledge she honored despite the nose dive her stock took. She did however, get a letter of admonishment from the FEC for securing close to four million in bank loans for her campaign and failing to disclose it. She won with less than one percent of the vote in 2000. Cantwell and Debbie Stabenow of Michigan were the first women to defeat incumbent Senators in their respective states. Later in 2006 Maria was re-elected by a sound margin of 16% points.

As junior Senator she has been consistently liberal. She voted against John Roberts as Chief Justice of the Supreme Court anticipating his views on abortion and the environment. She is against the privatization of Social Security and a strong supporter of environmental issues.

Senator Cantwell has been endorsed by the League of Conservation Voters, the Sierra Club, and Defenders of Wildlife Conservation fund for her opposition to ANWR drilling, for co-sponsoring the Roadless Area Conservation Act, and sponsoring the Clean EDGE act of 2006 to investigate alternative energy sources. (Senator Cantwell has been quoted as saying *"conservation must be more than an convenient slogan."*) She is the chair of the Senate Democrats 20/20 Energy Independence Campaign and co-chair of the Apollo Alliance. She helped pass legislation to prevent energy market manipulation and was one of only 34 Senators to vote against the Partial Birth Abortion Act of 2003. She voted for the original Iraq war resolution in 2002 while issuing a press release stating she felt there were certain questions the Bush administration had failed to answer.

She originally endorsed Hillary Clinton's candidacy but on Clinton's concession she offered her support to Obama saying, *"I do want to see a strong Democratic woman in the White House...that's why I'm so glad Michelle Obama will be the first lady."*[41]

Cantwell who declares herself to be "100% pro-choice" has a ranking of 100% with NARAL on exactly that issue. The LCV also gives her 100% on environmental legislation and the APHA does for public health policy. HRC gives her 89% on gay rights and the NAACP gives her 93% for pro affirmative action while the ACLU gives her only 60% for civil rights. The COC gives her 39% for pro-business legislation

---

41 Niki Sullivan (2008-06-15). "", The News Tribune

and CATO gives her only 42% for free trade. The AFL-CIO gives her 85% on union issues, and the ARA gives her 90% for seniors issues. CAF, gives her only 67% though, for energy independence. She has a rating of 0% from the USBC on being tough on illegal immigrants, (and as could be predicted by being 100% pro-choice,) the Christian Coalition gives her voting record 0% as well.

Senator Claire McCaskill, Missouri

"I just want to make sure that they feel comfortable that I am ready to take these folks on, that I am ready to be on their side, that I can do this. And that means listening to them and reassuring them that I'm not going to be afraid to say no to anybody in my party, anybody in the Republican Party or any lobbyist."

- Claire McCaskill

Junior Senator Claire McCaskill of Missouri will be the Senior Senator of her state when Senator Kit Bond retires in 2010. She was the first woman Senator from Missouri to be elected in her own right and was another of the seventeen women the New York Times cited as most likely to be the first woman President of the United States.[42] Claire's mother was the first woman elected to the City Council of Columbia Missouri and her father served as a state Insurance Commissioner under the Governor. Senator McCaskill has a B.A. in political science from University of Missouri and received her J.D. University of Missouri Law School in 1978. After graduating law school, she spent a year as a law clerk with the Missouri Court of Appeals and then joined prosecutor's office in Jackson county specializing in arson cases. In 1982 she successfully ran for office in the Missouri House of Representatives becoming the first female attorney to serve there in forty years. She served in the Missouri House from 1982 until 1986 and was the first Missouri state lawmaker to give birth while in office. From 1989 to 1991 she worked as a private practice trial lawyer. She was elected to the Jackson County Legislature, (similar to a County Council office) in 1990. In 1992 she was the first woman elected to be the Jackson

---

42 Zernike, Kate (2008-05-18). "", *New York Times*

County Prosecutor and was re-elected in 1996. In 1998 she was elected to be Missouri's second woman State Auditor.

She was the Democratic candidate for Governor in 2004 and lost to the Republican Secretary of State 51% to 48%; in her twenty years of public service it was the first time she lost an election. In 2006, she won her bid for the Senate by a narrow margin. Senator McCaskill has denounced the use of era marks and pork barrel spending and along with Russ Feingold is one of only two U.S. Senators that pledged to *never* use earmarks. After the Walter Reed scandal erupted Senator McCaskill introduced legislation with then Senator Obama demanding accountability for agencies tasked with the physical and mental care of wounded veterans. She supports embryonic stem cell research but not cloning. She supports a ban of partial birth abortion but supports emergency contraception and voted no on barring minors from passing state lines to get an abortion, and voted no on rescinding funding to organizations that support abortion. She supports energy independence by 2020 through the use of alternative fuels, and that global warming should be taken into account in federal planning but still supports subsidies for oil and gas companies. She voted against free trade with Peru and supports a ban on Argentine meat imports to prevent the spread of hoof and mouth disease.

She voted to expand the SCHIP program to provide health insurance for an additional two to four million children and voted for an increase in the tax rate on individuals earning more than one million a year. She does not support amnesty for illegal immigrants or a guest worker program. She supports improved mental health care for war veterans and voted yes for limiting troop deployments to twelve months at a time. She currently serves on the Senate Armed Forces Committee, the Senate Commerce Committee, the Senate Homeland Security and Government Affairs Committee, the Senate Indian Affairs Committee, and the Senate Aging Committee. After only a few years in the Senate she hasn't racked up extensive ratings with all of the various organizations and interest groups. She was one of the first Senators to endorse Barack Obama's presidential nomination, inspired by her daughter's interest in the Obama campaign, and was a big help in his narrow victory in the Missouri primary. Here's a angry quote from Claire when financial institutions who had received some of the $700 billion bailout from Congress used the money to pay bonuses to top executives:

"We have a bunch of idiots on Wall Street that are kicking sand in the face of the American taxpayer.......They don't get it......You can't use taxpayer money to pay out $18 billion in bonuses."

Then Senator McCaskill introduced a bill to limit compensation at any company receiving bailout money to $400,000, saying, *"We should have done it in the first place. But I don't think any of us thought these guys were this stupid. I don't think any of us believed that they would take billions of dollars in bonuses while their institutions were literally days from being wiped out. But they did. And we've learned our lesson."*

The new bill which strengthens oversight of the $700 billion was a bi-partisan effort with Republican Senator Chuck Grassley of Iowa and was signed into law by President Barack Obama in April '09.

Senator Lisa Murkowski, Alaska

"I'm excited about what I have to offer. Not only a little bit of youth, but also a different perspective as a woman."

- Lisa Murkowski

Senior Senator Lisa Murkowski from Alaska is the first woman ever elected to either house of Congress from Alaska and also the first Senator *born* in Alaska. She earned her B.A. in economics from Georgetown University and her J.D. from Willamette University College of Law in 1985. Her father Frank Murkowski was elected to the U.S. Senate in 1980. From 1985 to 1998 Lisa Murkowski practiced law in Alaska becoming a member of the Alaskan Bar Association in 1987. In 1990-1991 she served on the Mayor's task force on the homeless. In 1998 she was elected to the Alaska House of Representatives and was named House Majority Leader in 2003. In 1999 she introduced legislation establishing a Joint Armed Services Committee. Lisa Murkowski sat on the Alaska Commission on Post Secondary Education chaired both the Labor and Commerce and Military and Veterans Affairs Committees.

In 2002 her father, Senator Frank Murkowski was elected Governor and in the grand old tradition of nepotism appointed his daughter to his vacated Senate position. Her response; *"In some people's mind the father-daughter connection is a liability. I am working very hard to let people know that I am not Frank Murkowski."* Another more blunt response on her part was, *"I have never once asked Alaskans to like how I got this job."* They may not have liked the way she got the job but some Alaskans at least must have liked her performance because she was elected in her own right in 2004. Senator Murkowski is known for being a pro-choice Republican. (which might explain why she wasn't a VP choice for the 2008 McCain presidential campaign, instead of the less-experienced, but pro-life Governor Sarah Palin.) She supports stem cell research and the expansion of the SCHIP to offer more children health insurance and is known to support health care reforms in her own state. This is motivated in part by sheer practicality; medical costs in Alaska, thanks to the remoteness of many of its towns, can be far higher than in the continental United States.

She is the vice Chair of Committee on Indian Affairs, a ranking member of the Committee on Foreign Relations, and also serves on the Committee on Health, Education, Labor, and Pensions, and the Committee on Energy and Natural Resources.

Senator Murkowski supports drilling in ANWR and has a 0% rating from CAF on energy independence and an only 11% rating from LCV on environmental issues. She has a 14% rating from NARAL on abortion rights and a rating of 83% from the Christian Coalition on her voting record. The HRC gives her 0% for gay rights and her 14% rating with the NAACP for affirmative action policies is barely any better. APHA gives her a 12% rating for public health and the NEA gives her 55% for public education. The COC gives her an 86% rating for being pro-business and the AFL-CIO gives her 15% for her union policies. The AU gives her 0% indicating she doesn't maintain much division between church and state and the ARA gives her 0% on her voting record regarding senior's issues. (Let's not forget the indigenous Alaskan population used to send their elders off adrift on icebergs and there may be some lingering cultural remnants from that time.)

Senator Jeanne Shaheen, New Hampshire

"Anyone who has spent time in New Hampshire has an emotional tie to the state ... but what I appreciated when I was governor was the

people, and I believe they are what made a difference in getting the peace treaty negotiations done. ... It's been the people — their independence, self-reliance and imagination. It's all possible in New Hampshire."

- Jeanne Shaheen

Certainly New Hampshire's Junior Senator Jeanne Shaheen is embedded deeply in the political roots of New Hampshire being the first woman in U.S. history to be elected both Governor **and** Senator of a state. Shaheen received her B.A. in English from Shippensburg University of Pennsylvania and her M.A. from the University of Mississippi where she taught high school for a while. In 1973 she moved to New Hampshire and again taught school. She worked on several campaigns for the Democratic party and in 1990 she successfully ran herself for the New Hampshire state Senate. In 1996 she became the first elected woman Governor of New Hampshire.

She was re-elected in 1998 and 2000. For her first 4 years as Governor Shaheen held true to her pledge not to raise taxes (New Hampshire has no sales tax and no state income tax). Th en in during her third term her proposal of a 2.5% sales tax was rejected by the state Legislature. She was considered in 2000 to be a possible vice-presidential running mate by the Gore campaign, but she informed them that while she was flattered by the attention they should look elsewhere to fill the spot.

In 2002 she declined to run for a fourth term of Governor but instead ran for the Senate and was defeated by John Sununu 51% to 47%. Later that year, a Republican consultant pleaded guilty to jamming phone lines the Democratic party had set up urging people to go to the polls, which some believe to be what could have cost Shaheen the election.

In 2004 she was named the national chairperson of John Kerry's Presidential campaign and is credited (for better or for worse considering Senator's Kerry loss) with securing him the presidential nomination. She had spent the two years prior to that teaching at Harvard University and in 2005 she was named Director of Harvard's Institute of Politics.

In 2007 she announced her intention to run **again** against John Sununu for the Senate seat he then held. She beat him by seven points and was sworn in on January 6, 2009. She received assignments to the Senate Foreign Relations Committee and the Senate Energy and Natural Resources Committee.

In her first floor speech Senator Shaheen urged for investment in clean energy as a way of combating the economic recession and bringing about energy independence stating *"these investments will create good jobs, help revitalize our economy, begin to curb global warming, and put us on the path to energy independence."*[43]

Senator Kirsten Gillibrand, New York

"As a ten year old girl I would listen to my grandmother discuss issues and she made a lasting impression on me."

- Kristen Gillibrand

Senator Gillibrand, the junior Senator from New York, and newest member of the Senate Women's club came to occupy her seat through special appointment like many of her predecessors have. (Though, in the past the vacancy in question was not because an elected woman to the Senate accepted the Cabinet post of Secretary of State.) At 42, Senator Gillibrand is the youngest member of the U.S. Senate and is the second female Senator in New York after Clinton. She was active in politics from an early age; while attending Dartmouth University she interned for Senator D'Amato and then earned her Juris Doctorate from U.C.L.A. Senator Gillibrand was Special Counsel to HUD Secretary Andrew Cuomo during the Clinton administration.

In private practice she was known for doing pro bono work for tenants in unsafe homes and abused women and for her representation of the cigarette manufacturer Phillip Morris whose employees bankrolled her Congressional campaign which she herself disclosed. She chaired the Women's Leadership Forum Network. She has hardly had time to accumulate any legislative record in the U.S. Senate but as a member of the House of Representatives she developed a reputation as a centrist Democrat. When President Obama announced Hillary to be his choice for Secretary of State Gillibrand was rumored to be one of several possibilities to fill the slot. The list included another famous woman Caroline Kennedy, (writer, attorney, and only surviving child

---

43 DiStaso, John <u>Shaheen, in Senate Debut, Urges Energy Investment</u> MSNBC 2:45 am ET, Sat, Jan 10, 2009.

of President JFK) as well as NY Attorney General Andrew Cuomo (son of former NY Governor Mario). This was quite a political list.

Given that Senator Gillibrand is of course representing the citizens of New York City, her appointment by Governor David Patterson was somewhat controversial in that she is considered to be more conservative than New York city Democrats generally are, and that she was from the less densely populated upstate area suggesting that Governor Patterson may have appointed her as a way of currying favor with her former district rather than respecting the wishes of the state of New York's Democratic party.

At the beginning of the 110th Congress she co-founded the Congressional High Tech Caucus. She'd ride the Washington Metro with her son Theodore dropping him off at congressional day care, before going to work where she served on the Committee of Agriculture and Committee on Armed Services. In her time in Congress she received a rating of 100 points from NARAL, the American Civil Liberties Union, the Alliance for Retired Americans, and the Children's Defense Fund. The NRA gave her a rating of an A, the Human Rights Council gave her a rating of 85%, the AFL-CIO a rating of 96%, the League of Conservation Voters 85%, the NEA gave her an A, the anti-immigration group Americans for Better Immigration gave her an B, and the NAACP gave her a rating of 96%. The Chamber of Commerce gave her 60%. To summarize she's usually pro-business, definitely pro-guns, and in favor of closing the borders with strongly liberal on reproductive rights, civil liberties, and affirmative action with a record of being pro-union and supporting environmental protections. Time will tell if that legislative record will continue in the U.S. Senate.

Secretary of State Hillary Clinton

"The challenge now is to practice politics as the art of making what appears to be impossible, possible."

- Hillary Clinton

No other Senator has been talked about as much as Hillary (over 50 books have been written about her, and she has written several herself.) Being First Lady for eight years put her very much into the public eye and under the microscope of the press, where she remained as a New York Senator and then throughout one of the most publicized and covered presidential races in American history. Now Secretary of State Clinton is no longer in the United States Senate, (her seat being now occupied by Senator Gillibrand) but we are including her profile here because former Senator Clinton is one of the most, if not the most important women politicians in the U.S. at this time.

Senator Hillary Rodham Clinton of New York made history for being the first female Senator elected from New York, the first former First Lady to be elected Senator, and, so far, the woman who has come closer to winning the White House than anyone else in history.

Secretary of State Clinton was the first student to deliver the commencement address at Wellesley College where she received her B.A. and then went on to earn her Juris Doctorate at Yale University where she met and married Bill. (Thus began what would become the most famous marriage of two politicians in U.S. History, for better or worse.) Secretary of State Clinton's work on family issues goes back over three decades; in 1977 she co-founded the Arkansas Advocates for Children and Families a non-profit organization advocating family friendly policy in Arkansas. She was First Lady of Arkansas 1979-1981 and 1983-1992 and then became First Lady of the United States of America from 1992-2000.

In 1994 she launched a plan to reform health care that failed for many reasons, the most important probably being the huge amounts of money and resources the health insurance industry mobilized against it. She was the first First Lady to be subpoenaed and brought before a Grand Jury, (not to mention all the conspiracy theories involving Vince Foster, lesbianism, witchcraft, etc.) but despite the fact that special prosecutor Kenneth Starr managed to spend $80 million in taxpayer money investigating the matter she was never charged with a single criminal offense.

As First Lady she advocated for the State Children's Health Insurance Program, (which at its time of creation was the largest tax-funded health insurance coverage for United States children since Medicaid was founded in the 1960's and within two years over one million children were enrolled) the Adoption and Safe Families Act, (to shift the focus on protecting children's health and welfare instead of re-uniting children with their biological families no matter what) and the Foster Care Independence Act that provides health insurance to former foster children under the age of 21 through Medicaid funds. She also helped form the Office on Violence Against Women in the Justice Department, hosted the first White House Conferences on Teenagers and first White House Conference on Philanthropy as well as conferences on child care and early childhood development.

She traveled to almost 80 countries setting a record as the most traveled First Lady (good Sec of State preparation). In the late 90's she was one of the early voices to speak out on behalf of Afghan women under the Taliban, before 9/11 made their plight fashionable.

After entering the U.S. Senate, Clinton joined the Senate Prayer Breakfast to form alliances with religiously inclined Senators and served on five committees; the Committee on Budget (2001-2002), the Committee on Armed Services (2003-2009), the Committee on Environment and Public Works (2001-2009), the Committee on Health, Education, Labor, and Pensions (2001-2009) and the Special Committee on Aging.

Not far into her 1st Senate term came the catastrophe of the 9/11 attacks. Along with Senator Charles Schumer from New York she helped secure 2.1 billion in funding for restoration of the World Trade Center after the 9/11 attacks and led the investigation into health issues faced by the 9/11 first responders. She strongly supported President George W Bush's Patriot Act(despite the fact that every civil liberty group in America raised concerns). She also supported the war in Afghanistan, and the Iraq War Resolution (which may have cost her the Democratic presidential nomination). She was solidly opposed, though, to most of President Bush's domestic agenda, voting against both his major tax cut programs, and against both John Roberts and Samuel Alito for the Supreme Court.

Hillary had been preparing for a Presidential campaign of her own for many years before the 2008 campaign and her popularity in New York and across the nation remained strong throughout the campaign as she added yet another "1st" to her list - she was now the first First Lady to run for the Presidency. There was a feeling by many that it was 'her time' to run and win, the front runner and favorite going in, she was "the person to beat", it was up to her to make mistakes in order to lose it. But in Barack Obama she faced another popular candidate who's time had come to rise with a message of hope and change in a terrible economy, a phenomenon. And after a long, sometimes bitter fight for the nomination against Senator Obama, she became an ardent supporter of his candidacy proclaiming, "*The way to continue our fight now to accomplish the goals for which we stand is to take our energy, our passion, our strength and do all we can to help elect Barack Obama*".

Apparently reconciliation between them was sincere; in November of 2008 he offered her the position of Secretary of State and she accepted leaving the Senate in 2009. So she is currently serving in one of the most high-profile and powerful Cabinet positions in the White House, and in another step in an amazing career she racks up another first; she's the first First Lady to hold the seat of Secretary of State.

51

WOMEN SENATORS ? UNIQUE CHALLENGES FOR WOMEN

CHAPTER THREE
THE PRESS - PUBLIC PERCEPTION

Because I am a woman, I must make unusual efforts to succeed. If I fail, no one will say, "She doesn't have what it takes." They will say, "Women don't have what it takes."

- Clare Boothe Luce, writer, Congresswoman

The emotional, sexual, and psychological stereotyping of females begins when the doctor says, "It's a girl."

- Shirley Chisholm, first black Congresswoman

Women are better represented in the Senate than ever before; the glass ceiling has certainly been cracked but it's by no means non-existent and Senator Clinton provides us with an excellent microcosm to examine the issue with. With 18 million votes Hillary came closer to the presidential nomination than any other woman in U.S. history; it was a truly historic and proud moment for feminism but at the same time many young women reported her candidacy as being eye-opening to them to the extent that sexism in our society still exists. A young college student interviewed by <u>Salon</u> detailed this phenomenon, *"When the election started, I felt very post-feminist," said Wiegand. "I felt like, I'm a woman and I'd love to have a woman president, but I also have many other issues I care about and the Iraq war is a big one, and I'm not going to make my decision just because I'm a woman." But over the course of the campaign, Wiegand said, "there has been a lot of anger toward Hillary that's felt really intense and misogynistic. The gloating after Iowa was something to behold. And it's made me realize we are still dealing with the gender issue. I don't think we know what to make of women in power, or make of Hillary. I don't think the world is as postfeminist as I was feeling that it was."*

What ultimately made such an impression on Wiegand and millions of other young women like her was not so much for the fact that Hillary Clinton lost the nomination, (she was after all faced with an extraordinarily charismatic opponent and her vote authorizing President Bush to go to war in Iraq was a millstone around her neck) as for the *tone* surrounding her candidacy in the media.

"*Women have very little idea of how much men hate them.*"
                                                    - Germaine Greer, writer, feminist

We think Germaine Greer was being overly fatalistic but nevertheless it was extremely disturbing to see the amount of sheer misogyny leveled at Senator Clinton. There was the infamous anti-Hillary Political Action Committee Citizens United Not Timid aka C.U.N.T. There were the popular anti-Clinton sites on Facebook including "Hillary Clinton: Stop Running for President and Make Me a Sandwich," and "Life's a Bitch: Why Vote for One? Anti-Hillary 08." Then there were the t-shirts, bumper stickers, and buttons being hawked by conservatives with such slogans as "KFC Hillary special, Two fat thighs, Two small breasts and a left wing." "Stop Mad Cow disease," - "No Hillary in 2008." Rush Limbaugh proclaimed that Americans just didn't want to see a sixty-something woman in the Oval Office because it wasn't "appealing." As Jessica Wakeman noted Hillary Clinton is probably the first presidential candidate to have hecklers yell at her, "Iron my shirt," and to have a pair of nutcrackers fashioned in her image. She was accused of being a radical hippie, a cynical opportunist, a lesbian, as a victim of her husband's notorious extra-marital affairs, or as an enabler of them. Her laughter was constantly described as a "cackle" no doubt to paint her as a witch while when she raised her voice it was described as "shrill" or that she was having a "meltdown."

It wasn't just from men either, commentator Jane Hamsher when critiquing one of the debates stated *"Hillary is obviously going after Obama, but somebody needs to remind her to smile when she does it."* Hamsher didn't, however, see fit to remind Obama or Edwards to smile when *they* went of the offensive. Randi Rhodes of Air America radio referred to her as "a big f*cking whore." !

New York Times opinion columnist Maureen Dowd was perhaps the worst of all in this regard, describing Senator Clinton as "unapologetically emasculating." Dowd has at times referred to Senator Clinton as a "nag" and a "witch" and compared her to the fictional character Carmela Soprano. At a particularly low point Dowd went so far as to liken Hillary Clinton to a science fiction monster, ""*It's impossible to imagine The Terminator, as a former aide calls her, giving up," Unless every circuit is out, she'll regenerate enough to claw her way out of the grave, crawl through the Rezko Memorial Lawn and up Obama's wall, hurl her torso into the house and brutally haunt his dreams.*" It eventually reached the point that the *New York Times* public editor Clark Hoyt after receiving numerous complaints by readers, concluded in a column that Dowd "went over the top." It's only a small consolation that Dowd has also used the same style and tone (not so much reporting, as caricatures and sometimes baseless character attacks using references to junk pop culture) when writing about Bill Clinton, Al Gore, George W. Bush, Dick Cheney, and others.

Senator Clinton is not Mother Theresa but the sheer level of vitriol she inspired seemed far out of proportion to her alleged sins; yes she has been known to get down and dirty in the political muck but she is by no means the <u>worst </u>among presidential candidates in that respect, (even her most negative campaign tactics against Senator Obama looked downright genteel in comparison to what the McCain/Palin ticket dished out,) and contrary to the conservative writings about her she's a political moderate, and while the Democratic base could not, (perhaps justifiably,) forgive her vote for Iraq, she has a great deal of other legislative accomplishments that were quite distinguished. Senator Clinton may not been the most deserving candidate for the Oval Office but she didn't deserve to be demonized either.

So why was she?

When Code Pink (the famous feminist anti-war campaign) was asked why they **specifically** targeted their protests at Senator Clinton for her voting for the Iraq War Resolution when there were numerous other Democratic Senators who had done the same they cited two reasons; she was unusually high-profile because of her presidential candidacy and because of her sex, "You expect more of a woman," as Zillah Eistenstein wrote to columnist Katha Pollitt. The clear implication then is that Eistenstein expects less from men. We have to wonder if men (including those who voted **against** that same Iraq War Resolution) might be insulted by, while the male Democratic Senators who voted **for** the war resolution were let off more easily because of their gender. The bottom line is that Senator Clinton was being held to a higher standard than any male politician would have been; even by a **women's organization!**

Again, **Why?**

The answer lies in the peculiar double bind that women in power face. Dr. Alice Eagly at Northwestern University has shown that people discriminate against female leaders because qualities stereotypically associated with women (nurturance) conflict with stereotypically masculine qualities associated with effective leaders (assertiveness). Women who display masculine qualities often achieve success but lose out in popularity.

Dr. Susan Fiske of Princeton University discovered similar results. Stereotypes about women fell into two categories, warmth and competence. The more "warmth" a woman was perceived as possessing the less competent she was judged while the more a woman was perceived as competent the less "warmth" she was seen to possess. In other words women could be perceived as either likable *or* capable but not both. Ergo, Senator Clinton's might well have inspired much of the antipathy to her not in spite of her impressive resume but indeed because of it. As former Congresswoman Patricia Schroeder noted, *"Many women have more power than they recognize, and they're very hesitant to use it, for they fear they won't be loved."*

This is not an issue for men who can easily imagine themselves as both powerful **and** beloved in the "benevolent patriarch" archetype. Moreover, perceptions of men's capabilities did not change if they fathered children whereas women after giving birth were seen as less competent which often led to them being steered into the infamous "mommy track," career wise. An impressive body of controlled experimental studies and examination of decision-making processes in real life show that, on the average, people are less likely to hire a woman than a man with identical qualifications, are less likely to ascribe credit to a woman than to a man for identical accomplishments, and, when information is scarce, will far more often give the benefit of the doubt to a man than to a woman.

Even in the area of science where one would think objectivity was a given, gender bias exists. A study by Jennifer Freyd of the University of Oregon gave college students identical scientific articles to be evaluated by specific criteria-one group received the article with a male name attached and the other with a female name. Articles believed to be written by women were consistently ranked lower than when these articles were believed to have been written by men. Men are presumed to be competent until they prove otherwise while women are perceived to be incompetent until proven otherwise. Charlotte Whitman famously said, *"Whatever women do they must do twice as well as men to be thought half as good. Luckily, this is not difficult."* may or may not have been right about the latter part but she wasn't (sadly) too far wrong about the first part.

"Well behaved women rarely make history."
> - Laurel Thatcher Ulrich, Harvard historian

This has profound implications for women entering politics who already have the deck stacked against them since voters of both genders will subconsciously be holding them to higher standards. If women candidates play up their knowledge and skills too much they will be seen as cold and well…bitchy, but if they work too hard at coming across as congenial and compassionate they will be seen as soft and weak. Their male competition on the other hand, can easily present themselves as both highly qualified and companionable. For male politicians it's often a huge asset to be seen as a "family man," though, bachelors running for office is hardly unheard of either, but a female politician's family could work against her while at the same time the *lack* of one could be pointed to as proof that she isn't a "real" woman".

Running for office is about "tooting one's own horn," and is the ultimate act in self-promotion but for women candidates it's far trickier. Dr. Laurie Rudman at Rutgers University found that individuals of both genders dislike self-promoting women far more than they dislike self-promoting men, and in fact that *men* were reluctant to hire self-promoting women **even when they believed the woman was competent.** Adlai Stevenson said that "the hardest thing about any political campaign is how to win without proving that you're unworthy of winning." Sadly, it seems that for a significant number of voters a woman might prove herself "unworthy" of political office by having the **temerity** to run in the first place!

> "*Men with average to below-average intelligence think that they are quite clever. And very smart women think their intelligence is low.*"
>
> - Adrian Furnham, psychologist

Another major issue is that women themselves (perhaps in part because self-promoting women are disliked) often tend to underrate their own abilities; while men often overrate theirs. Adrian Furnham a professor at University College London analyzed some thirty studies on IQ and gender; he found that men and women were approximately equal in terms of intelligence.[44] He found that women tended to underestimate their own IQ's by about five points while men tended to overestimate theirs. "Even women themselves consistently tended to overrate male brain power while underrating that of other women, and parents generally seemed to consider their sons brighter than their daughters"; even though as Furnham noted girls were regularly outpacing boys in nearly all subjects at the UK. (Maybe their parents simply thought that the academic performance of their children was unrelated to intelligence?)

This is troubling for what sorts of messages these parents send to their daughters; messages they absorb their whole lives. (It may not be in the son's best long term interests either to breed a false sense of

---

44 He's Not as Smart as He Thinks He Is, Joan Raymond Newsweek Net Exclusive Jan 23 2008

arrogance/hubris.) Generally speaking in job interviews it's important to radiate self-confidence; this goes doubly so if the "interview" is a political campaign. The very act of running for office takes a great deal of confidence that many women have been socialized *not* to possess. Former Governor of Vermont Madeline Kunin whenever she brought up the notion to her female students that they someday might follow in her footsteps was always hearing the women second guess themselves. They made comments like these:

"I'm always doubting myself, and when I'm proven wrong, I don't digest it."

"I don't want to come off as a person who knows it all."

"I like the idea of being involved but not running. I think there is arrogance, a certain public persona that you have to take on to go through the whole election process;"

NY Congresswoman Carolyn Maloney has asserted that the biggest problem for young women trying to break into the political scene is that they lack the "chutzpah" displayed by so many young men.[45] She related the following scene:

"In my first race for Congress, I had two opponents in the Democratic primary: an obscure attorney who wasn't a factor in the race and Abe Hirschfeld. Abe was an eccentric multimillionaire who had made a fortune building parking garages and fitness clubs. He eventually bought the **New York Post,** *which barely survived his tenure. Right after I announced my candidacy, he asked me out to lunch. It seemed like an unusual request, but I always like to size up my opponents. I had barely started to dig into my salad when Hirschfeld revealed the purpose of the meeting: he said he believed that in order to beat Republican congressman Bill Green, Democrats needed to unite behind one candidate - him. He asked me to drop out and endorse him. I'd been serving in elected office for a decade. I had worked in public service for almost my entire career. He had been off*

---

45 Reports of Our Progress Have Been Greatly Exaggerated Maloney, Carolyn, Modern Times NY, NY 2008 pg 217

*building parking garages and fitness clubs. And **he** was asking **me** to drop out of the race!"*

Lest we chalk up Abe Hirschfeld's strong sense of entitlement **solely** to the notorious levels of hubris possessed by the very rich it's been noted by many others in the political sector that while women always seem concerned they're "not ready" for office their male counterparts on the other hand, just tend to "go for it." An important study conducted by Brown University concluded that men **are more than 35% more likely** than women to consider themselves as political candidates and this gender gap persisted across the board regardless of political party, religion, race, ethnicity, income level, or age. Men were 65% more likely to rate themselves as "very qualified" to run for office while women were twice as likely to rate themselves as "not at all" qualified to run for office. More than 80% of men reported themselves as ready to do the job as an office holder, while less than 2/3 of the women did and women's doubts about their qualifications played nearly twice as large a role as that of men in reducing their chances of considering candidacy.

These gender difference did **not** stem from differences in experience with the political arena - the men and women in the sample were about equal in their attendance of political meetings, observation of legislative processes, interaction with elected officials, and serving on the boards of non-profit organizations and foundations. More importantly the study discovered that *"Women's tendency to underestimate their political qualification also does not reflect their concrete credentials, on which they are well matched with the men in the sample."* The women were just as qualified to run as the men; they just didn't **know** it. As Representative from California Loretta Sanchez once put it, *"When you ask a man to run, he says, 'Okay, but the party is going to have to do this for me, and the party is going to have to do that for me, and you are going to have to throw a fundraiser for me.' When you ask a woman to run, she says, 'Do you think I'm qualified?'"*

Perhaps one reason that women often **don't** think they're qualified to run for office is because they're not **asked** to. Another finding in the Brown study was that the men were significantly more likely than the women to be recruited for to campaign for political office, (43% of men as opposed to 32% of women,) especially by political actors whose encouragement was the most likely to be taken seriously. Needless to say, having other people encourage you to run is a huge impetus to do so. The Brown study found that "When a respondent receives external support to run from both a political actor and a non-political source the likelihood of considering a candidacy more than doubles. Women's likelihood of considering running increases to 0.75: and men's probability of considering a run increases to 0.85."

"Some of my friends and fellow campaign workers came up to me and said, 'You're very good at this. Have you ever thought of running yourself?' Of course, I didn't. But suddenly I found myself thinking, 'They're right, why not?"

- Senator Mary Landrieu (D-LA)

This is particularly surprising because the study had also concluded that for most general elections women stood as good a chance at winning as their male counterparts despite the problems of sexist attitudes we've discussed! Yet **both** political parties have been lackluster in their attempts to groom women candidates. Some of this may be internalized gender stereotyping; party insiders when they're trying to decide who to recruit ask themselves, *"Who's the best **man** for the job?"* This sort of sexism is of the genuinely unconscious and often subtle variety but other times it's considerably more blatant. Vermont Representative Rachel Weston when introducing herself to another Representative old enough to be her father was told by him that he would have liked to have been introduced to her with her clothes off.[46] (Misogyny dies hard particularly among the older generation.) Or sometimes it may be party insiders falsely believing that a women candidate wouldn't be as electable, perhaps one reason for Abe Hirshfeld's unusual lunchtime proposal to Carolyn Maloney. It's to counteract this problem that such groups as Emily's List and The White House Project exist to get more women into the political arena.

---

46 Kunin pg. 80

"I've yet to be on a campus where most women weren't worrying about some aspect of combining marriage, children, and a career. I've yet to find one where many men were worrying about the same thing."
- Gloria Steinem, feminist, journalist

Many young women who might otherwise consider beginning the path to public office are dissuaded by their belief that such a career is incompatible with a family life. (Aspiring male politicians on the other hand tend to assume their **wives** will be able to pick up the slack.) Certainly the demands of political campaigns and holding public office can make for a difficult balancing act nevertheless many female politicians have done it though, their methods vary.

"My advice to women who don't want to become involved in public service because they have children is that it's not that hard to do both. You can juggle it. You may not have the most traditional lifestyle."
- Congresswoman Deborah Pryce (R-Ohio)

Speaker Nancy Pelosi didn't start her political career until her children were older and she believed didn't need her at home so much anymore. When Hillary Clinton was First Lady she had a tiny private kitchen in the White House for family meal time together. (It's worth noting that by the time Hillary began running for office in her own right her only child Chelsea was an adult.) Senator Mary Landrieu of Louisiana kept her family in Washington D.C.; she and her husband owned a house four blocks from her office in the Senate saying "It's the only way I can do this job and be a good mother to them. I put my children to bed almost every night, and they wake up to their mother's voice every morning. Nothing would separate me from that." Other female politicians such as Congresswomen Maloney, Bean, and Wasserman Schults, shared a house together in D.C. and would leave their families in their home districts and go home every weekend while using cell phones and email to be in constant contact throughout the day.

Senator Amy Klobuchar of Minnesota credited her spouse for making the juggling act possible, "My husband is incredibly helpful," and recounted that he had the distinction of helping plan the Laura Bush luncheon, and was the only husband to be consistently involved in the Senate spouse group.[47] It is not for nothing that Michigan Governor Jennifer Granholm when giving advice to other women who considered following her example said, "I hope you have all married well. If it weren't for my husband, I wouldn't be able to do it."

Certainly an interest in politics would be a good reason why a young woman when choosing partners should focus on those potential suitors who believe in shared parenting responsibilities and are **not** wedded to traditional family roles; it's perfectly possible to be a good wife and a great mother while holding public office but it's not possible to be Donna Reed at the same time. Let it not be thought, though that it's an absolute essential to even be married in order combine parenting with political office. Senator Claire McCaskill of Missouri, was a single mother for seven years after her divorce, before she remarried. Her first run for office (as state auditor) took place when she was a single mother of young children, and she depended greatly on the support of her family, particularly her sister to help her out. She claims though, that in some ways political office actually eased the difficulties in (by necessity after her divorce,) being a mother with full time employment, "*There are several things about this career that are counterintuitive. One is that it's so difficult to have a family if you go into politics. I will give you that there are times it is, but there are many times that this career provides much more flexibility than a traditional nine-to-five job. Your bosses are the people. If I wanted to take a morning off to be the homeroom mother for the Valentine's Day party at my children's school, I did it. I also had to work nights and weekends sometimes, but ultimately you have the flexibility.*"

A number of women who've held political office note that a side benefit of their public duties was that their children learned to be more self-sufficient; they knew their mothers would always be there for them when the chips were really down but that they couldn't just call mom and ask her to drop everything and bring a forgotten notebook to school. Studies have consistently found that children of mothers who are gainfully employed outside the home are more likely to hold egalitarian gender roles and be more independent. It is true that when mom's a Senator the children's lives are subject to attention by the press that might well be unwanted but that particular problem goes as well

---

47   Kunin pgs 109-113

for the children of male politicians and is certainly something that should be carefully considered by aspiring public servants of **both**.

An even more difficult issue is that of having children while *in* office. Governor Jane Swift (D-MA) who was the first Governor to give birth while in office, created a nationwide controversy when she took several months maternity leave after the birth of her twin daughters, though, she continued to exercise executive authority at the time including chairing a meeting of the Massachusetts Governors Council from her hospital bed. She also notoriously breast fed her infants in her office as well. This led to questions about whether Governor's Swift's pregnancy and subsequent status as a new mother were compatible with the duties demanded in her office; even from self-described feminists such as Wendy Kaminer of <u>The American Prospect</u> who stated on the topic of Swift's husband taking over as a stay-at-home dad, "*he can't bear them for her; he can't recuperate from childbirth for her (if recuperation is necessary); he can't experience whatever hormonal swings lay in store for her, catch up on her sleep for her, or keep her from being happily distracted by the mere thought of her two new babies. Why would you want to become governor and give birth to twins more or less simultaneously, anyway?*"

Certainly Ann Crittenden had a point when she decried the concept of "childbirth as appendectomy," and the idea that it would only take a few weeks to "recover' from a new baby, but still it's hard to think of a single case of a male politician being criticized for having family responsibilities that *might* come into conflict with the responsibilities of office. You never hear commentary like, "Senator Robert X already has four children under the age of 10 and his wife is pregnant again; how can he possibly expect to juggle being a dad to five young kids with serving his constituents?"

Our new President Barack Obama while making his historic run for the presidency was required to spend much of the past two years on the road and often had to cope with long periods of separation from his wife Michelle, and daughters Sasha and Malia during that time, but this in fact was perhaps the one aspect of Obama's history and family situation that did **not** become the focus of intense media debate. However, Michelle Obama (who wasn't even running for any political office) was often the focus of a lot of scrutiny and criticism as being "untraditional" First Lady material. Maureen Dowd took Michelle

Obama to task in her columns for her noted sarcastic wit, *"I wince a bit when Michelle Obama chides her husband as a mere mortal—— comic routine that rests on the presumption that we see him as a god ... But it may not be smart politics to mock him in a way that turns him from the glam JFK into the mundane Gerald Ford toasting his own English muffin."*[48]

This of courses raises the question - why on earth we would think less of our political leaders for apparently being able to prepare their own food instead of needing other people to do their toasting for them?) Michelle Obama has sometimes been labeled "an angry black woman," not because she was particularly intemperate, but because she had a habit of speaking her mind about the heated issues her husband's candidacy provoked. Once again, we are left to conclude that it is minority women who have the hardest time of it in the political arena.

Interestingly enough, while Michelle Obama has been known to criticize some of Senator Clinton's tactics and policy decisions she specifically named that other notoriously "untraditional" First Lady as an example of a political spouse she admired noting that Senator Clinton despite the incredible difficulty of parenting an adolescent girl under a media microscope her child had turned out to be an exceptionally grounded young woman,[49] something Michelle Obama as the mother of two daughters could appreciate and look to as inspiration. Michelle had during her husband's presidential race made a commitment to only be away from home once a week on the campaign trail and to never stay away more than two days from their children, always arriving home by the end of the second day.[50] It's also likely that Michelle Obama an attorney herself with a keen interest in public policy had a certain professional respect for Senator Clinton as well. And while we cannot speculate as to whether Michelle might wish to emulate Hillary Clinton and Elizabeth Dole with a run for the Senate she would certainly have both the advantage of precedent from both, Senator Clinton and former Senator Moseley Braun, as well as a competitive resume on her side.

Another bind for women is the "damned if you do, damned if you don't" attitude towards "femininity" in women politicians that is

48 Dowd, Maureen (2007-04-25). "". #
49 Karen Springen (October 2004). "", *Chicago Magazine*
50 "". *Pasadena Weekly* (June 5, 2008

practiced even by self-described feminists. When Pelosi was sworn in as Speaker of the House she highlighted her experiences raising five children and asking her grandchildren to appear on stage with her; this prompted Katrina Van Heuvel the then editor of *The Nation,* to write on her blog, "*I wonder why Pelosi, a woman I admire, seemed so keen to use her first day as speaker to portray herself as a traditional, family-first kind of woman.*"

Perhaps Pelosi was as Van Heuvel suggested cynically trying to play herself as maternal as a method to make, herself seem more "acceptable" as a female politician but it's also equally possible that Speaker Pelosi wanted to share this moment with her family. Is a woman who highlights her family life "betraying" feminist ideals by "conforming" or is she just like all the male politicians who know that showing a happy stable family life is a great way to humanize themselves to voters? Lest anyone conclude that the path for female politicians is to cultivate a decidedly **non-maternal** mystique female politicians are routinely penalized for that as well. Elizabeth Edwards, wife of Democratic presidential candidate and Senator John Edwards(North Carolina) saw fit to tell a luncheon by the Ladies Home Journal that she felt her "choices" had made her "happier" and more "joyful" than had Senator Clinton's. (Elizabeth Edwards gave up her legal career to support her husband's ambitions and care for her family unlike Senator Clinton who most decidedly did **not**.)

We would never presume to judge Elizabeth Edward's choices or her happiness because of them but it does seem unfair then that she was willing to publicly judge Senator Clinton's (who never did so with Elizabeth Edwards). As Katha Pollitt put it, "*It is sad to think that Ms. Edwards would play the happy-homemaker card to help her* **lightweight** *husband best a woman with about ten times as much political experience. We all know Edwards did such a great job running for Vice President--the man was everywhere!--and made such a fantastic impression in his debate with Dick Cheney. Still, I might have gone for him in the 2008 primary, because every now and then he pops up out of nowhere and says poverty is bad. Now I dunno. We bitter ambitious career women have to stick together.*"[51]

---

51 Pollitt Katha *HRC Can't Get No Respect* The Nation November 6, 2006

This paradox goes for the other trapping of "femininity" as well. Senator Clinton was at one time deciding to do a photo shoot for Vogue magazine, but then missed the scheduled shoot because her advisors feared it would make her appear "too feminine." Anna Wintour the editor in chief of *Vogue* responded with a blistering editorial in the February issue proclaiming, *"Imagine my amazement, then, when I learned that Hillary Clinton, our only female president hopeful, had decided to steer clear of our pages at this point in her campaign for fear of looking too feminine. The notion that a contemporary woman must look mannish in order to be taken seriously as a seeker of power is frankly dismaying… This is America, not Saudi Arabia."* This was a fair critique on Wintour's part; why should a female politician be restricted to pantsuits simply in order to be taken seriously? Moreover, Senator Clinton was ironically enough often being derided as too "mannish."

But her advisor's fears were not entirely out of fantasy land either; witness the public brouhaha over the fact that in one of Senator Clinton's public appearances on the presidential campaign trail people could discern visible cleavage. A google search for "Hillary Clinton and cleavage," yields 167,000 results; with the first one being an "expose" by *The Washington Post*. It's hard to imagine something of **less** importance in a presidential campaign than a candidate's neckline, but nevertheless one of the largest and most prestigious papers in America considered the matter newsworthy.

Perhaps most depressing of all was the sheer amount of debate that was going on period over Senator Clinton's choices in clothes, make-up, and hairstyle instead of her policy positions. Female politicians are well aware that they are graded far more on issues of personal appearance than their male counterparts; something that is not only trivial and unfair but often quite exhausting. To prove it try the simple exercise yourself of going to the women's section of a department store and finding sets of clothing that are businesslike but not mannish and feminine yet not overtly sexual or "frilly" and see how long that task takes you; (men are included in this experiment) and that's not even including the personal grooming factor yet!

"I'm not saying the wife has to divorce her ethically challenged spouse, although, come to think of it, that would make a change. But just once I'd like to see her skip the press conference and fly off to Paris instead. And then

I'd like to see a political husband stand by his wife when she's caught, oh,
I don't know, giving a no-show job to her tennis instructor. Except that
particular shoe never does end up on the masculine foot, does it?" [52]

The last area of double standards for female politicians is in the area
of sex scandals. Women politicians are not immune to scandalous affairs
of course; U.S. Representative from Idaho Helen Chenoweth in 1998
(after running advertisements decrying President Clinton) admitted to
having had a six year affair in the 80's with a married man who later
worked on her Congressional staff. And State Representative Katherine
Bryson of Utah was caught with her lover on a surveillance tape by her
then husband, (who unlike most political wives later divorced her.) But
the number of women politicians who get caught in such sex scandals
isn't comparable to the number of male politicians, and the scandals
themselves don't seem to reach the same level of salaciousness.

There really isn't a female counterpart to former Governor of New
York Elliot Spitzer who prosecuted prostitution rings while engaging the
services of high end escorts to forego the use of condoms during their
sexual encounters, or Congressman Mark Foley's pursuit of teenage
pages. (This many wags have claimed is one of the best arguments for
increasing the number of women in politics it being especially unlikely
for a female politician to be able to conceal an illegitimate love child as
John Edwards allegedly did for sheer logistical reasons.)

Some have suggested this phenomenon can be traced back to the fact
that women are less biologically hardwired for adultery; since studies
have demonstrated though, that women are about as likely to cheat as
men are in a marriage this theory seems shaky. (Though, women are
far FAR less likely to frequent prostitutes be they gay or straight which
might go a long way toward explaining why we have yet to hear of any
women in either body of Congress being caught in a bordello's black
book.) Far more probable is the contention that women, particularly
women in public office, anticipate harsher consequences for adultery
than men do.

To look at an example from across the Atlantic, when the British
politician Edwina Currie published her diaries in 2002, she revealed that
she had a four year affair with her Conservative colleague John Major.
This brought a round of condemnation on top of her; a newspaper poll

---

52 Pollit Katha John Q Public *The Nation* March 13, 2008

showed that 88% of people thought it was wrong of her to reveal the affair and half of them thought the less of her for it; but only a third of those readers thought the less of **him.**[53] Once again when women are held to a higher standard the men get an easy pass of "boys will be boys." When men like Elliot Spitzer and the Republican Junior Senator of Louisiana David Vitter were caught frequenting prostitutes Their careers experienced diff erent levels of trouble, (Governor Spitzer was forced out of office which did not happen to Senator Vitter despite the fact he made "family values" a benchmark for his campaign) but *both* their wives swallowed their pride and stood by their sides to support them at press conferences. It's hard to imagine that in the (admittedly unlikely) event that Senator Vitter's counterpart Senator Mary Landrieu was somehow exposed as paying for the services of a male gigolo that her husband Frank Snellings would endure that same sort of public humiliation; he might be down at the bar or seeing a divorce attorney, and nobody would blame him.

Writer for *The New Yorker,* Henrick Hertzberg claimed the Elliot Spitzer scandal shouldn't have been a scandal in the first place since "no hypocrisy" was involved, (what did he make of the fact that Spitzer had sought jail time for some prostitutes when he was Attorney General while apparently hiring others?!?) and Alan Dershowitz opinionated, *"Big deal-married man goes to prostitute. In Europe this wouldn't even make the back pages of the newspaper."*[54]

Notice that Dershowitz said married **man** without stating whether he thinks this same "live and let live" attitude would apply to the sex lives of prominent married **women.** This double standard has been noticed and lambasted by a number of feminists, such as Debbie Walsh the director of the Center for American Women and Politics, *"They have put these women through so much already - it just seems to be a second level of humiliation, It is supposed to make him look like not such a bad guy. Like, 'Geez, look, his wife was standing next to him.' But in this case, she looked so pained that, to me, he looked less sympathetic,"* and Pam Gutwold communications professor from Penn State who exclaimed, *"I saw that and I wanted to yell at her 'You don't have to do this! Go*

---

53 Baird, Julia <u>Girls Will Be Girls</u> *Newsweek*, March 31, 2008

54 Stanley, Allesandra "<u>Mars and Venus Dissect the Spitzer Scandal on the Tv Talk Shows</u> *The New York Times*, March 12 2008

shopping! Go for a walk. Do anything else."[55] Still, generally speaking the "stand by your man" routine is considered almost mandatory for politician's wives but has never been dreamt of for political husbands. Not that we are suggesting that political husbands should follow the example of their female counterparts but that maybe political wives should take a lesson from the political husbands sparing themselves at least one public ordeal in the process.

Governor Spitzer's wife Sidra on top of everything else had to cope with prominent radio talk show host Laura Schlessinger suggesting that this was somehow **Sidra's fault**, "*Yes, I hold women accountable for tossing out perfectly good men by not treating them with the love and kindness and respect and attention they need.*" [56] (Yes the same Laura Schlessinger who was reportedly unfaithful in her first marriage and caused the breakdown of her second husband's first marriage, and bore a child with that same second husband out of wedlock, might just have personal reasons for choosing to blame *the spouse who was cheated on* rather than the *actual cheater*.) Apparently the fact that Sidra Spitzer gave up a successful career as an attorney to support her husband's ambitions and raise their three children was **not** sufficiently sacrificial enough on her part.

It's even been implied that Senator Clinton drove her husband to his well publicized extra-marital affairs by being insufficiently "womanly," before anyone jumps on that bandwagon it's worth noting that political wives of the more "traditional" bent from Wendy Vitter to Elizabeth Edwards have also had to cope with the discovery of adultery regardless of whether they stayed at home or not. Still this is yet another issue for women in politics; if their husband engages in adultery or any other unseemly behavior it reflects very badly on them and while male politicians have a similar problem to some extent with their wives it isn't nearly as prevalent because voters are more likely to perceive a wife as being a husband's "puppet" than vice versa.

The personal state of a politician's marriage is really no one's business but that of the married couple themselves, but the fact that the family as a whole may have a conflict of interest on certain policy matters is

---

55 Garofoli Joe "Why do political wives stand by their man?" *The San Francisco Chronicle,* March 12, 2008
56 Stanley, Allessandra "Mars and Venus Dissect the Spitzer Scandal on the Tv Talk Shows *The New York Times,* March 12 2008

worthy of public attention. So the fact that so much attention is given to Senator Clinton's spouse Bill Clinton, (who by way of being a former President himself was going to be incredibly high-profile no matter what the circumstances) having certain fi nancial interests abroad that could conflict with foreign policy issues is not in and of itself unwarranted. It **would** be completely inappropriate for Bill Clinton to be garnering large speaking fees from foreign nations or domestic special interest groups if his wife was in the White House as President or as Secretary of State which is why he's been asked to resign these fees once she's in office. Nor was it necessarily unfair that Vice Presidential candidate Geraldine Ferraro came under fire for her husband's financial dealings and failure to publicly release his tax statements, but it **is** unfair that Dick Cheney's wife Lynne's board membership at Lockheed Martin and other professional dealings **didn't get the same level of scrutiny**. After all Lynne Cheney's income from dealing with defense contractors is family income just as much as Bill Clinton's is; if it's improper for the goose it's improper for the gander.

So, do we set the standards too high and expect too much from women in public office? Or are we just not expecting *enough* from the men? Either way, in spite of the unfairness and inequity of treatment that this chapter speaks of, women are proving more each year that they can, and will, rise above it all and still reach their goals! And the proof is that the number of women in government keeps increasing. Even against all odds they are continuing to gain seats.

As readers may have noticed we are not discussing what was the "traditional" route for political office for women of special appointment or the "widow's benefit." It is true there was a time when women had little hope of reaching the Senate without being appointed by a man but those days are thankfully gone. (Though, sadly, even today the special appointment system helps.) It was necessary at one point to rely on special appointments to set the precedent and to let voters see that women could serve honorably in the Senate without any appearances by the Four Horsemen of the Apocalypse but women in politics no longer need that type of affirmative action.

Even Senators Caraway and Chase Smith who began their political careers by appointment were able to win elections in their own right later on. It is women like them that paved the way for Senator Clinton, possibly one of the most routinely disparaged women in American politics to win her New York Senate in her own right and be re-elected as well. Which is why it was more than a little insulting, for Caroline Kennedy and her supporters, when, lobbying Governor Paterson for the Senate seat that Hillary Clinton was vacating, to suggest their examples were equivalent. Senator Clinton may not have held *elected* office before she took her Senate seat but she did have to convince her "bosses" the voters of New York to give her the job and then convince them she'd done a good enough job in the first term to be given a second term as well. Journalist Lisa Belkin implied that Caroline Kennedy's seeking special appointment to the Senate was a form of "opting in" aka a woman who took time off to raise a family trying to restart her career,[57] comparing her to other working mothers in that regard. Besides the absolute absurdity of comparing Caroline Kennedy with her family connections to the situation of other stay-at-home mothers interested in re-entering the workforce Belkin was ignoring such figures as Speaker of the House Nancy Pelosi, another stay-at-home mom at one point who when she decided to enter politics still deigned to roll up her sleeves and *run*. (She was able to make a successful run by paving the way with years of service to the Democratic party apparatus in her area.)

Of course there remained the need to fill Senator Clinton's Senate seat by special appointment, (whether the special appointment system should be in place to begin with is a question for another time) and there might still be a nice symbolic value in appointing another woman to the post and definitely value in replacing Senator Clinton with someone with similar political views. (If for no other reason than the citizens of New York would not feel they were cheated by getting someone completely different from whom they originally elected in office.) But it's worth noting that Governor Patterson had a number of other Democratic women he could appoint to the office who had previous legislative experience including Senator Gillibrand who eventually was given the job. (Though, this choice was not without controversy of its own; Senator Gillibrand had direct political experience but was from upstate rather than New York City and was considered by many

---

57   Belkin Lisa <u>The Senator Track</u> *The New York Times Sunday Magazine* December 31, 2008

New York Democrats to be too conservative; there were a great deal of murmurings that this was a misguided political ploy on the part of the Governor who should have appointed Representative Carolyn Maloney or former Representative Elizabeth Holtzman.) The whole debacle as well as the Blagovich scandal was an excellent argument to the effect that rather than using "special appointments" to promote women, African Americans, sheep herders, rich scions of political families or what have you the best way to handle a vacancy in the Senate is with a special election so that whoever wins be it a man or a woman will have the credibility of having gotten their seat openly with a public mandate.

51 ?
IF WOMEN RULED THE WORLD, HOW WOULD THEY REPRESENT US?

CHAPTER FOUR

"If women ruled the world, the laws of the United States (and other countries) would respond better to the needs of the people and be negotiated in a more collaborative and less overtly partisan, competitive way. A good example of women working toward this goal of collaborative solutions is the group of female representatives in the Senate who meet monthly to negotiate legislation they can all support, setting partisanship aside."

- Joan Byrna Micehlson, CEO of Micheslon/Cooper Marketing in Las Vegas and Public Policy Chair, National Association of Women Business Owners.

"We'll be the first to admit…we think women can and should change the world."

- Thalia Zapatos & Elizabeth Kaufman, authors

February 26, 2008 was the date Dee Dee Myers' new book, *"Why Women Should Rule the World.,"* was released. Dee Dee Myers argues that there *are* certain intrinsic differences between women and men, and that it is precisely because of those innate differences that women should be in charge. She states that politics would be more civil, businesses more productive, and communities healthier and more wholesome because women are superior listeners, communicators, and consensus builders. She argues this is not just a product of socialization on the part of women but that of biology as well; that women are simply genetically hardwired to be more empathetic and communicative than men, though, perhaps less good at spatial skills.

"Women are not inherently passive or peaceful. We're not inherently anything but human."

- Robin Morgan, feminist, activist, writer

Dee Dee Myers' book is problematical from several angles. From a pragmatic attitude while Myers may think she is improving the odds for women to get ahead in practice in practice she may be just further inflaming the tiresome gender wars that have been such an impediment to political progress over the years and prevent men and women from finding common ground. Author Virginia Woolf noted in "<u>A Room of One's Own,</u>" that "All this pitting of sex against sex, of quality against quality; all this claiming of superiority and imputing of inferiority belong to the private-school stage of human existence where there are sides, and it is necessary for one side to beat another side." Moreover, there's considerable reason for skepticism about Myers' essential premise. For every scientific study that Myers can point to showing the differences between "Mars" and "Venus" brains there's a study showing that the two genders are more alike than different and that individuals tend to vary more than genders do.

As early congresswoman Rebecca Felton demonstrated, being a woman (and for that matter considering her success on the lecture circuit, a great communicator as well) by no means immunizes one to the worst sort of bigotry and hatred. In modern day times, Secretary of State, Condoleeza Rice has certainly not been an exemplary model for building international consensus and cooperation and in fact has been one President Bush's most loyal and ardent supporters of war. Small wonder then that noted feminist columnist Katha Pollitt once stated that, overall, she gives a candidates gender only 2% for overall importance in whether or not to vote for them. (Admittedly 2% could *still* swing a close call.)

"Can you imagine a world without men? No crime and lots of happy fat women."

- Nicole Hollander, cartoonist

Nicole Hollander was being funny but she wasn't accurate. Admittedly, women as a group are far less prone to violent crimes than men are which could perhaps demonstrate an innate spirit of gentleness or cooperation but this may be more an indication that women possessing less physical strength and being socialized for "niceness" simply don't have the same *opportunities* for violence as a group that men do. There are still plenty of individual women, though they are seriously outnumbered by their male counterparts who have nevertheless been capable of acts as violent and horrific as any male criminal ever devised. Writer, activist Barbara Ehrenreich noting the participation of women in the depraved acts at Abu Ghraib proclaimed, "*What we have learned, once and for all, is that a uterus is not a substitute for a conscience and menstrual periods are not the foundation of morality. That doesn't mean gender equality isn't worth fighting for, for its own sake. It is. And I will keep fighting for it as long as I live. If we believe in democracy, then we believe in women's right to do and achieve whatever men can do and achieve, even the bad things. It's just that gender equality cannot, all alone, bring about a just and peaceful world.*" And the author Deborah L. Rhode noted that "*Some of the worst voting record's on women's rights belong to women.*" It is all too human to internalize prejudices against oneself or worse yet "sell out" members of a fellow group to win approval from the more dominant members of society. As Frank O'Connor put it "no man is as anti-feminist as a really feminine woman."

The fact that women cannot depend solely on a candidate's reproductive organs to determine their voting pattern is also reflected in the attitudes of women voters; Journalist Sherrye Henry an unsuccessful candidate for the New York Senate in 1990; commissioned a national study on the attitudes of women voters to women candidates. Over 700 women voters were surveyed and 69% of the respondents said the candidate's sex made *no* difference to them. They were no more likely to vote for a woman than for a man; (someone perhaps should have brought this to the attention of the campaign strategists who thought that Sarah Palin would draw women voters back to the GOP.)

However, Dee Dee Meyers is certainly correct in one aspect; there's a great deal of evidence that women in elected office do <u>not</u> govern in precisely the same way as their male peers, and more equitable representation of women, (those eventual fifty-one Senate seats for instance,) could indeed result in significant legislative differences. Indeed the behavior of the women currently serving in the United States Senate helped inspire Dee Dee Myers to write her book. To begin with, the women presently in the Senate have already enacted huge changes in society. Olympia Snowe, while in the House of Representatives first lobbied to include women in more clinical drug trials and health studies, noting one infamous example in particular of a *breast cancer* study where all the test subjects were *men*. Nor is, it coincidence that funding for breast cancer research was greatly increased after the "Year of the Woman"(1992). When a commander who had been involved in the infamous Tailhook scandal sought to retire at four stars it was Washington Senator Patty Murray and the other women in the Senate who challenged it; it didn't stop the commander from retiring with four stars but it certainly made a statement; and not one that everyone felt comfortable with. Now that women were in the Upper Congressional House, sexual harassment issues were no longer something that could be quietly swept under the carpet.

It cannot be said that the gender ratios of the Senate are the *sole* determinant in legislation regarding so called "women's issues", nor even the most *important* factor; nevertheless even an increase in the *visibility* of women in office makes, a difference in how often issues affecting women and families are addressed. In 1969 there was only one woman, Senator and *no* bills on women's issues were introduced in the Upper House. In 1993 the number of women in both houses of Congress nearly doubled and some *357* bills on women's and family issues were introduced in the Senate; 230 of these bills having been introduced by men. [58] As Kay Bailey Hutchison explained it, *"when I'm asked, "Does it make a difference that women are part of the process?" I say "You bet. We bring our life experiences to the table. Nobody fought for homemakers to have retirement accounts until we did in the Senate in 1993, for God's sakes.,"* later adding, *"It wasn't that men were against these changes. They just hadn't considered the issue before because they hadn't*

---

58 Foestel pg. 3

experienced the problem in their own lives. As women have become a part of the system, that's changing."[59] When Nancy Pelosi was inaugurated to Speaker of the House, she like many past speakers thanked her family for "their love, support, and the confidence to go from the kitchen to the Congress." What was different was that no past Speakers (who were all men) had ever mentioned the kitchen in their inaugural address nor did they make a point of having their grandchildren surround them on the podium.

Senator Kay Bailey Hutchison has discussed another change in the system as well, "In previous years, when I have run for office, I always had to overcome being a woman. All I've ever wanted was an equal chance to make my case, and I think we're getting to that point-and that's the victory."[60] This observation is supported by evidence, as Dee Dee Myers noted, "Once a state has elected a woman to the legislature or the statehouse or the Senate, it is more likely to elect another one. And another one."

"Whether women are better than men I cannot say-but I can certainly say they are no worse."

- Golda Meir, former Prime Minister of Israel

It's perfectly human and understandable to vote according to what one knows from personal experience and for a politician to focus on those issues he/she has seen with their own eyes. However, when all politicians are only a certain segment of the population at large then they are going to vote what issues *they* know personally and so even if these politicians are not *intentionally* discriminating or marginalizing the groups that are not being represented certain issues just might not occur to them. And the historical differences, between "women's work" and "men's work," do affect what issues the two genders feel are most important just as the experiences of black people living in the inner cities gives them a different perspective on issues of law enforcement and education than those held by white people in the suburbs.

---

59 Whitney pg. 53
60 Lauren Whittington, "Women See Gains Slowing: Number of Female Lawmakers Not Expected to Rise Dramatically," 19 September 2002, 13, 20.

"I am working for the time when unqualified blacks, browns, and women join the unqualified men in running our government."
- Cissy Farenthold, attorney, educator, Texas State Representative, Vice-Presidential candidate

This is of course an argument not just for greater representation of women in the U.S. Senate but for blacks, Hispanics, Asians, and for greater economic diversity as well instead of having the Senate essentially made up of affluent white men; which regardless of the individual merits of the particular affluent white men in question that are serving office is bound to skew the viewpoint as a whole towards the values and traditions of well...affluent white men and is one reason why the Senate is considered somewhat more elitist and "clubby" than the House of Representatives which is significantly more diverse.

A good example of how this can work in practice is that right-handed people often design instruments that are almost impossible for left handed individuals to use-and it's only after left-handed persons complain that a version for them is added. (Or alternatively when left-handed people, become, involved in the design process.) It's highly doubtful that anyone ever said or even thought, "Oh, let's just forget about women in all health studies-they're only half the population you know!" but more likely that doctors, public health officials, and legislators all being male themselves never thought twice about the fact that everyone in the test studies was male; but it was something the women who joined the Senate couldn't help but notice. (note- while 50% of the population are women only about 10% are left-handed.)

As former Governor of Texas Ann Richards put it, "It is not that women are better than men...but I hope we all accepted long ago that we are different. The most sympathetic and sensitive of our men friends, no matter how hard they try, cannot hear with a women's ear of process information through a woman's experience." This went beyond the issue of test studies; as Senator Patty Murray stated, "Before I went into the U.S. Senate there was very little funding put into breast-cancer research, but when six women were elected into the U.S. Senate in 1992, we forced money for research." When women in the United States are the most likely in all, the world to get breast cancer and when American women have a 1 in 8 chance of developing invasive breast cancer this was no small thing on the part of Senator Murray and her colleagues. Nor is it a coincidence that 1993 that the Family and Medical Leave Act which was first introduced in 1986 wasn't passed until 1993; after it had been championed by the new Senator Murray.

Besides, life experience there is the fact that many women serving in the two houses of Congress received considerable support both financially and in grass roots efforts from such organizations as Emily's List that explicitly campaign for women candidates to support issues dear to women voters. The old expression, "You have to dance with them what brung you," applies to politics as much as ever it did and it applies equally to both genders.

In a society where women are usually the primary caregivers for children it's not at all surprising that a poll by Lake Research for Center for Policy Alternatives found that 63% of women as opposed to only 41% of men thought more should be done to expand the availability of good quality affordable child care in the United States-a nearly 20% gap. Polls have found women to be consistently more concerned with issues related to education and also to health care; a reflection of the fact that women in American society are not only more likely to bear the brunt of responsibility for children but also for elderly, disabled, or sick family members as well. A nationwide poll by Garin-Hart-Yang Research in May, 2005, had the following results; "When asked what their greatest concerns were, women voters identified Social Security (27 percent), followed by the war in Iraq (25 percent), and healthcare (20 percent). When asked whether the statement, "Taking care of the needs of other people is the most important role I play," described them well, 46 percent of women voters said yes. But only 24 percent of men said that description fit them."

This went on to have an effect in the 2006, Congressional election where women were significantly more likely to vote in Democrats rather than Republicans. In Virginia, 55% of women as opposed to 45% of men voted for Democrat Jim Webb. In Missouri, 51% of women but only 46% of men voted for Democrat Claire McCaskill. In Montana, 52% of women compared with 48% of men voted for Democrat Jon Tester. In all three races, the stronger support among women tipped the tide in favor of the Democratic candidate. In New Jersey and Maryland, the incumbent Democratic candidates Robert

Menendez and Benjamin Cardin both maintained their seats because of their strong support among women rather than men.

Some experts think the differences in male and female voting patterns go beyond a few isolated issues into a greater psychological divide as to the whole nature of what government should be; with women supporting a "nanny state" aka, an government that seeks to shelter and provide for its citizens while men support a "daddy state," or a government system that put greater emphasis on law and order, respect for hierarchy, and aggressive military action. A recent Rasmussen poll to determine who Americans considered to be the most influential president of the 20th Century with the choices being Presidents Franklin Delano Roosevelt author of "The New Deal" and the social safety net as we know it and President Ronald Wilson Reagan champion of small government and the winner of the Cold war; they found that among male voters Reagan was the favorite by 46% to 42% but among women voters Roosevelt was the favorite by a whopping fifteen points.[61] It was a stark illustration of the gender divide that rules in politics.

The National Election Studies conducted a total of 11 surveys between 1982 and 2004 asking the question, whether government should be providing more or fewer services. American's preferences overall for government services varied substantially over the years with a low number of 31% in 1982 and a high of 50% in 2004, (which many observers, attributed to worsening economic circumstances and a rise in health care costs) but the gender gap on the question remained relatively consistent with women on average favoring increased government services by 10 percentage points. The American National Election Studies polled Americans on their perceptions of presidential candidates in 2000 and 2004; in both election cycles women were more likely to agree that the Democratic presidential candidate was a "strong leader" who "cares about people like you."

The gender gap on the issue of whether it is government's responsibility to provide health care did not emerge until 1988, and it is less of a gap than that for general social services but nevertheless, women favor government assistance in health care by 5 percentage points over men and there's evidence the margin may be increasing.

---

61   Rasmussen Reports Saturday, December 27, 2008

Women on average are ten percentage points *less likely* to support the death penalty and are more likely to support gun control. The NES when surveying on the issue of defense spending between 1980 and 2004 found that men on average favored increasing the defense budget by 8 percentage points over women. (Perhaps women favoring increased social services just thought the money was better spent on student lunches rather than bullets.) Polls during the 90's found that women were on average 5 percentage points less likely to favor the use of force in solving international crises than men.

A Gallup poll in 2003 (at the height of the Bush administration's propaganda campaign trumpeting Saddam's supposed links to Al Qaeda and stockpiles of chemical weapons) found that while both men and women generally favored the Iraq war, support among men was 12 points higher; 78% of men compared to 66% of women. By 2006, when support for the Iraq war had plummeted study after study confirmed that women considered the Iraq war to be the most important issue of the Congressional midterm election over men by 10 percentage points. The National Organization of Women(NOW) had opposed the Iraq war since 2002 before it actually began, arguing that *"women bear additional personal costs in patriarchal wars that ruin their country's physical infrastructure, destabilize their economy, destroy their homes and kill and maim children and families. Eighty percent of the world's refugees and displaced persons are women and children. Women are victims of increased sexual abuse in areas of conflict and in the military, as we have seen here at home at military bases and recruitment centers, and in Iraq. Sexual violence and abduction of women and girls increase significantly under military occupation; perpetrators are rarely apprehended and prosecuted in such violent and hostile environments.*

- Statement of NOW Executive Vice President Olga Vives

NOW was in the minority at the time they first opposed the Iraq war, but they were remarkably prescient not only in the matter of public opinion which has become increasingly opposed to the war in Iraq but to the fact that Iraqi women according to many humanitarian groups on the scene have been the biggest losers among the civilian population since the war began seeing a complete reversal of all the rights they enjoyed under Saddam and now under constant threat of kidnapping by "rape gangs." [62] For too many years, the plight of women in wartime or under certain regimes was considered a somehow "separate" issue of one specific interest group instead of a vital measure of how a good half of the human population in any given area was faring; thanks to the work of groups like NOW and other feminist organizations that take an international perspective to women's empowerment that has begun to change.

And it's worth noting that Senator Clinton (despite her many welldocumented other issues and her sometimes aggressive tactics against Senator Obama in the Democratic nomination process) has long been a champion of women's rights abroad from when she was a First Lady. She gave a speech at the Fourth World Conference on Women in Beijing criticizing China's record on women's rights proclaiming, "that it is no longer acceptable to discuss women's rights as separate from human rights," despite pressure from the Chinese to soften her remarks. She was one of the most prominent voices against the repression of women in Afghanistan under the Taliban long before 9/11 made the issue fashionable in the United States and helped found Vital Voices an international initiative sponsored by the U.S. to promote women's political participation in their own countries. Her domestic record has been equally if not more impressive; as a First Lady she championed the State Children's Health Insurance Program, successfully lobbied for increased funding for prostate cancer and childhood asthma at the National Institute of Health, helped create the Office of Violence Against Women, initiated the Adoption and Safe Families act, and helped pass the Foster Care Independence Act, as well as hosting numerous family and children conferences at the White House. In her role as Senator, she and Senator Schumer secured over 20 billion in funding to rebuild the World Trade Center site and took a leading role in investigating the health issues faced by 9/11 first responders. Senator Clinton co-sponsored the 21st Century Nano technology Research and Development Act and led a bipartisan effort to bring broadband to rural communities, as well as working with Republican Senator Majority Leader Bill Frist in support of modernizing medical records with computer technology to reduce errors. She has served on five Senate committees and nine Senate subcommittees including

62 Iraq: Decades of suffering, Now Women Deserve Better. Amnesty International

the Committee on Health, Education, and Labor and the Special Committee on Aging and has generally enjoyed high approval ratings her time in the Senate.

Interestingly enough during the 2008 presidential race there was concern in certain circles that former Clinton supporters embittered by the perception that their candidate was victimized by sexism (which she was just as Senator Obama was the victim of racism in such primary states as Pennsylvania) would cast their votes for John McCain. Whatever truth there was or was not to this concern, ten of the Democratic women in the Senate made an urgent appeal to counteract that including an "checklist for change" in the next election that included such obvious issues as equal pay for women and affordable health care as well as environmental protection, economic measures to keep jobs in America, and providing benefits for military veterans. Certainly, while women in the U.S. Senate then take an interest in more traditionally "feminine" issues it is by no means the *sole* focus of their concerns which vary according to the constituencies they represent.

Now comes, the ultimate question for women voters regarding women candidates. Does greater representation of women in political office then, translate into better legislation and policy for women *generally*? The answer is most definitely **yes**, even granting that not all women politicians are crusaders for so-called "women's" issues while many male politicians have been. The Institute for Women's Policy Research did a study on women's representation in government across all fifty states and then checked those results according to which states had the best records on women's issues. To better understand these results, the women's issues they were looking at were based on the Platform for Action at the Fourth World Conference for Women in Beijing and covered the areas of violence against women, welfare and child support collection, women friendly employment corrections, legislation protecting sexual minorities, and reproductive rights. They found that in general states with higher representation of women had more women friendly policies. In the tables below you can directly compare the states by representation of women vs. women friendly policies.

Table 1. State Ranks & Composite Scores for Women in Elected Office, 1996

RANK	STATE	SCORE	RANK	STATE	SCORE
1	Washington	2.96	26	North Dakota	1.47
2	Kansas	2.90	27	New Mexico	1.44
3	Colorado	2.88	28	New York	1.43
4	Alaska	2.73	29	South Dakota	1.43
5	Hawaii	2.60	30	Missouri	1.42
6	Delaware	2.50	31	California	1.37
7	New Jersey	2.35	32	Wisconsin	1.34
8	Indiana	2.33	33	Utah	1.32
9	Minnesota	2.31	34	Pennsylvania	1.31
10	Arizona	2.16	35	Iowa	1.28
11	Vermont	2.13	36	Massachusetts	1.23
12	Nevada	2.03	37	Texas	1.21
13	Connecticut	1.97	38	Florida	1.19
14	Ohio	1.94	39	Tennessee	1.15
15	Michigan	1.92	40	Oklahoma	1.12
16	Idaho	1.89	41	Georgia	1.03
17	Oregon	1.80	42	North Carolina	0.99
18	Maryland	1.78	43	Arkansas	0.98
19	Illinois	1.77	44	Virginia	0.88
20	Rhode Island	1.63	45	West Virginia	0.82
21	Wyoming	1.59	46	South Carolina	0.77
22	Maine	1.58	47	Alabama	0.68
23	Montana	1.52	48	Louisiana	0.61
24	Nebraska	1.51	49	Kentucky	0.55
25	New Hampshire	1.51	50	Mississippi	0.52

Source: IWPR's 2000 report on *The Status of Women in the States*

Table 2. State Ranks & Scores for Women's Rights & Resources Checklist, 2000

RANK	STATE	SCORE	RANK	STATE	SCORE
1	Hawaii	26.99	26	Kentucky	13.63
2	Vermont	23.63	27	Montana	13.52
3	Washington	23.48	28	Ohio	13.18
4	California	23.47	29	Utah	12.59
5	Alaska	22.73	30	Colorado	12.57
6	New Jersey	21.43	31	Delaware	11.89
7	Connecticut	21.27	32	Nebraska	11.54
8	Massachusetts	20.99	33	Oklahoma	11.36
9	New York	20.42	34	Arkansas	11.25
10	Illinois	19.88	35	Florida	10.91
11	Rhode Island	19.67	36	Georgia	10.61
12	New Mexico	19.66	37	Kansas	10.41
13	Maryland	19.22	38	Michigan	10.41
14	Iowa	18.74	39	South Carolina	10.22
15	New Hampshire	18.33	40	Louisiana	10.21
16	Minnesota	18.01	41	Arizona	9.95
17	Oregon	17.75	42	South Dakota	9.90
18	Nevada	17.69	43	North Carolina	9.44
19	Wisconsin	16.21	44	Alabama	8.84
20	Pennsylvania	15.64	45	Virginia	8.44
21	West Virginia	15.42	46	North Dakota	8.42
22	Maine	15.23	47	Indiana	8.05
23	Texas	14.87	48	Idaho	7.48
24	Wyoming	13.73	49	Mississippi	6.58
25	Missouri	13.64	50	Tennessee	6.35

Source: IWPR's 2000 report on *The Status of Women in the States*

Here we have the exact issues on which the states were being graded on.

Table 3. Indicators of Women-Friendly Policy: Women's Resources and Rights Checklist, 2000

Violence Against Women

Number of states in which domestic violence is a separate criminal offense:30

Number of states with laws requiring domestic violence training of new police recruits:.. 32

Domestic violence and sexual assault spending per person: $1.34

Number of states in which a final stalking offense is considered a felony: .. 10

Number of states with laws requiring sexual assault training for police and prosecutors:... 10

Child Support

Percent of single-mother households receiving child support or alimony:34%

Percent of child support cases with orders for collection in which support was collected: 39%

Welfare Policies

Number of states that extend TANF benefits to children born or conceived while a mother is on welfare:.. 27

Number of states that allow receipt of TANF benefits up to or beyond the 60-month federal time limit:.. 30

Number of states that allow welfare recipients at least 24 months before requiring participation in work activities:... 23

Number of states that provide transitional child care under TANF for more than 12 months:... 33

Number of state TANF plans that have been certified or submitted for certification under the Family Violence Option or made other provisions for victims of domestic violence: 40

In determining welfare eligibility, number of states that disregard the equivalent of at least 50 percent of earnings from a full-time, minimum wage job:... 25

Average monthly TANF benefit, 1997-98: $358

Employment/Unemployment Benefits

Number of states with minimum wage higher than the federal level as of January 2000:... 10

Number of states that have mandatory temporary disability insurance:....... 5

Number of states that provide Unemployment Insurance benefits to:

Low-wage workers..12

Workers seeking part-time job..9

Workers who leave their jobs for certain circumstances ("good cause quits") 23

As of July 2000, number of states with proposed policies allowing workers to use Unemployment Insurance for paid family leave:..0 Enacted; 12 Proposed
Number of states that implemented adjustments to achieve pay equity in state civil services: 20

Sexual Orientation and Gender Identity
Number of states that have civil rights legislation prohibiting discrimination on the basis of sexual orientation and/or gender identity:......................... 19
Number of states that have a Hate Crimes law covering sexual orientation:24
Number of states that have avoided adopting a ban on same-sex marriage: 20

Reproductive Rights
Number of states that allow access to abortion services:
Without mandatory parental consent of notification.............................9
Without a waiting period..33
Number of states that provide public funding for abortions under any or most circumstances if a woman is eligible:... 15
Number of states that require health insurers to provide comprehensive coverage for contraceptives: 11
Number of states that require health insurers to provide coverage of infertility treatments: 10
Number of states that allow the non-biological parent in a gay/lesbian couple to adopt his/her partner's child:.. 21
Number of states that require schools to provide sex education: 18

Institutional Resources
Number of states that have a Commission for Women: 39

For sources and more information on the indicators used here, see IWPR's 2000 Report on The Status of Women in the States.
Compiled by the Institute for Women's Policy Research.

The Institute for Women's Policy Research found after analyzing the data that essentially for every one point increase in a state's score for elected women in office means an increase of nearly 3.5 points in a state's score on the Women's Resources and Right's Checklist. Now some might question whether causality is demonstrated by this graph; isn't it possible that states are generally more interested in women's issues and the increased representation of women in their governments is just an effect of that rather than the *cause* of the legislation? This question obviously could only be answered by looking at the specific actions of women legislators on such policy issues.

"Through an analysis of post-*Webster* abortion bills it was found that women representatives secure committee assignments that allow them to block pro-life legislation. This is especially pronounced in states with few women legislators and states most likely (according to other studies) to support policies restricting choice." [63]

The flip side to this was demonstrated recently in the depressingly juvenile behavior of members of House Caucus, (Democrats no less!) when debating Obama's stimulus bill which happened to include money set aside for family planning and birth control. You would not think it would be too hard to understand why in times of economic crisis a lot of lower income families might consider it especially important not to have an unplanned for pregnancy at that time but apparently many people (including Fox anchor man and TV host Chris Wallace) have trouble differentiating individual decisions about birth control that just happens to be purchased with Medicaid funding with China's mandatory one-child policy. Many members of the Congressional Caucus, "*acted like they were in junior high,...not only did they not understand this issue, but they are uncomfortable even talking about it.*" They simply couldn't stop snickering whenever the words "stimulus" and "family planning" were used in the same sentence. (God forbid they ever be invited to a scientific conference involving the "big bang" theory.)

A congressional staffer there, made the following observation, "*These issues are second nature to the majority of women in Congress, so when we talk to women members or their staffers about the connection between family planning, and women's economic security, they don't need an explanation. They just get it. Many of the men, however, do not. It is clear we need to educate them. If they don't understand the issues, they won't be able to defend them effectively.*" [64] One possible form of education might be to find a way to suggest women's access to contraceptives could have an impact on the sex lives of **men;** not only have male legislators of both parties have been diligent in promoting that Viagra and other erectile dysfunction drugs be covered by both Medicaid and private

63 Berkman, Michael, and Conner, Robert, *Do Women Legislators Matter?* Politics Research, Vol. 21, No. 1, 102-124 (1993)

64 Jacobson Jodi, *Lessons From the Stimulus Debate: Sex Ed for Talking Heads, Male Lawmakers*, RH Reality Check, January 29, 2009-8:00 am.

insurers but the CIA used Viagra as an incentive to buy the loyalty of local tribal chiefs in Afghanistan.[65]

Nor does this rule apply solely to abortion, birth control, or other issues that are seen as somehow exclusively "feminine". Women legislators are more likely than their male colleagues to oppose government funded school vouchers, the death penalty, and a constitutional amendment to allow prayer in public schools. Democratic women outnumber Republican women 61 to 39 percent and Democratic women are much more likely to identify themselves as "liberal" than Democratic men 40 to 23 percent.[66] Women legislators have been found to be more likely to vote the liberal or moderate side on policy issues such as hate crimes, affirmative action, and civil marriage for gays and lesbians. As former Vermont Governor Madeline Kunin noted, "Many women feel a special responsibility to become advocates for these issues, but not for these issues alone." This was borne out in a study of the 103rd and 104th Congresses done by the Center for American Women and Politics that concluded, "Most congresswomen, Democratic and Republican, believe they have an obligation to represent women." A national survey of women and men legislators done by the Center for American Woman and Politics at Rutgers University found that a *majority* of both male and female legislators agreed that the increased presence of women has helped broaden citizen access to government particularly among economically disadvantaged groups. The CAWP also found that women legislators are more likely than men to report that citizens are very helpful to them; reflecting either that ordinary citizens are more likely to initiate contact with women legislators, (perhaps feeling they are "softer" or less intimidating than their male counterparts,) or that women are more likely to reach out to ordinary citizens.

U.S. Representative Melissa Bean told the Chicago Herald in 2005, "Many of the issues that women address are important to all, but often led by women. Education, environment, and health care, tend to be championed by women in government because they are more intimately involved in the schools and the parent-teacher organizations." Representative Nydia Velazquez of New York, stated "Before I came

---

65 Warrick, Joby, *CIA Buys Afghan Chief With Viagra* <u>Washington Post</u>Friday, December 26, 2008

66 Kunin pgs 91-92

here....I saw that women's issues were not part of the national agenda. So it is our responsibility to participate in every single issue that we have here and every debate that we have here....If we don't force others to focus on women's issues then it will not be a part of the debate." This also applies to outreach for international women's programs; some years ago the sixteen women serving in the Senate met with the women leaders in Northern Ireland to discuss strategies in bringing civil peace to an country that had been torn apart by warfare. It was also the sixteen in the Senate who passed a resolution condemning the brutal regime in Burma for its suppression of democracy demonstrators; actions like these are what have convinced so many like Dee Dee Myers and NOW that greater representation of women in the Senate would mean more emphasis on peace and diplomacy and less war-mongering.

It's dangerous to over-generalize about such complicated questions but the fact remains that women voters are consistently more dovish than men and assuming then that women Senators were representative of American women than they too would be more likely to favor diplomacy over aggression in foreign policy issues. Women are also more likely than men (for better or for worse) to report that the attitudes and opinions of their constituents would be their primary consideration in determining their votes by 42 percent to 33 percent.[67]

Given the fact that women are generally more in favor of civil rights for gays, affirmative action programs, and tend to be more likely to believe the government should help the needy it's not surprising that a study by the Eagleton Institute for politics concluded that "a large majority of women legislators, as well as a majority of male legislators agree that the increased presence of women in the legislature has made a difference in the extent to which the economically disadvantaged have access to legislatures and the extent to which legislatures are sympathetic to the concerns of racial and ethnic minority groups." One factor behind that of course might well be because women (only earning 71 cents to a man's dollar) are significantly more likely to have personal experience with being "economically disadvantaged," especially if they have children.

In fact studies have consistently shown that having children is arguably the most financially costly decision any woman can make in

---

67 Kunin pg 92

terms of earning power over her lifetime; in great part because of the difficulties of finding affordable quality child care. Male pundits and politicians often dismiss child care policy in the U.S. (or our country's notable lack of one) as a side bar or a "soft" issue but the effects it has on American families cannot be overestimated. It impacts the decision of many women whether to have children at all, how many children to have, family finances, and of course domestic stress levels.

These effects ripple through society as a whole but it is women with children who see the primary shocks to hit the water and thus for whom the issues becomes one of grave importance. Because of that fact interest in the issue tends to cross party lines among women; when the Family Medical and Leave Act came before Congress half of Republican women voted for it compared to only 27% of Republican men; in the meantime *every* Democratic congresswoman voted yes but 13% of Democratic men said no. The bipartisan Women's Caucus introduced 70 bills in 1993 alone related to matters such as women's health, domestic violence, and educational equity. This sort of bipartisan cooperation has applied to other areas besides stereotypical women's issues as well; when the Omnibus Crime bill came to the floor in 1994 with a ban on assault weapons it was supported by 40 of the 48 women of the House and 6 of the 7 women in the U.S. Senate.

Now American women are not by any means uniform in their opinions and neither are the current women Senators, nor would that be the case for all future women in the Senate; nor *should* it be. But the simple math of the matter means that in a Senate with **51** women the majority of female Senators as the majority of American women and who had the support of some like minded male colleagues would be enough to tilt the votes on a number of bills. This could make for dramatic differences in our country but they would in a sense be differences that were *restoring* equilibrium to a nation where a disproportionately male governing body was disassociated from the values and concerns of a slight *majority* of the population.

Let's say there was a bill earmarking a huge expansion in funding for daycare subsidies and centers in a Senate where there were **51 women Senators**; 30 women support it and the other 21 do not. The 49 male legislators are split almost evenly with 27 opposed to the bill and 22 in support of it. The 22 men who support the expansion in funding added to the 31 women who supported it equal 52 votes which allow the bill to go through. In other words women Senators could be the swing voters on a number of such issues *even if* the women do not always agree or even have an iron hard majority of agreement to make the crucial difference. Besides the example of child care, this could impact on issues as diverse as criminal legislation, environmental protection, gay marriage, health care, and military spending.

Besides the legislative issues there is also the matter of presidential appointments; most notably the Supreme Court. The President of the United States is allowed the privilege of nominating judges to the highest Court of the land but these nominees still have to pass through the U.S. Senate. So far Justices Sandra Day O'Connor and Ruth Ginsberg have been the *only* women to ever serve in this most powerful of branches. During her confirmation hearings Justice Ginsberg she looked forward to seeing "three, four, perhaps even more women on the high court bench, women not shaped from the same mold, but of different complexions."

Sadly, we are not some ways away from realizing Justice Ginsberg's dream or realizing Justice O'Conner's wishes when she said in interviews, "I hope there will always be women, plural, on this court."[68] When Justices William Rehnquist and Sandra Day O'Conner, (famously the first women *ever* appointed to the Supreme Court,) retired, President George W. Bush nominated two highly conservative white males who were both appointed. This left the U.S. Supreme Court with only one woman justice and eight men; does it seem likely that this would have played out exactly the same as it did in a Senate with **51** women? Does it seem likely that President Bush would have even *tried* to appoint an conservative white man with noted anti-abortion views to replace the legendary swing vote of Justice O'Connor one of only two women justices to ever serve in the highest court of the land with **51 women Senators** in the first place?!?

Women do not and should not vet candidates based solely on gender but they are not likely to buy the argument that a qualified woman candidate could not be found for such a vital government branch which was already so lopsided in gender representation. As the Lilly Ledbetter case demonstrated the stakes are too high for that.

---

68 Kunin pg 75

With Supreme Court Justice David Souter's recent retirement announcement and President Obama's nomination of Sonia Sotomayor as Souter's replacement we can hope again for a second woman on the Supreme Court. Sometimes gradual progress means a few steps forward, followed a step back before we're ready to step forward again.

51 ?
WHEN ?
HOW WOULD THEY
REPRESENT US ?

CHAPTER FIVE

One of the county commissioners in my district said, "It will be a cold day in hell if that woman becomes a state legislator." After I won, my dad said, "Well I guess you're going to have to go buy him a coat."
- Washington State Rep Cathy McMorris

"For all the hype over 18 million cracks in the glass ceiling (referring to Clinton's supporters,) until we have around 267 cracks in the U.S. Capitol, we still have a way to go".
- Laura Russell, News Editor <u>Montana Kaimin</u>

Senator Barbara Mikulski, when giving her endorsement to her colleague Senator Hillary Clinton's candidacy for the Democratic Presidential nomination, besides noting Clinton's leadership skills explicitly referred to a desire to break one of the few remaining glass ceilings in government by electing the first female president. Obviously, a desire to make history by electing the first woman, or the first black man, or the first *black woman* to be the Commander in Chief should not be the only consideration for putting someone into the White House, but there's no denying the psychological allure of helping break down the walls as being a *factor* in the decision process in dealing with a situation where there's more than one acceptable candidate. Political progress after all is something that tends to start out slowly but then gain momentum; even ten years ago for a black man with the middle name "Hussein" even being a presidential candidate much less win would have been considered outlandish. Fifteen years ago, having nine women in the U.S. Senate was considered extraordinary and today there are seventeen.

When only 38 women in U.S. History have served in the U.S. Senate the fact that almost half that number are currently serving shows that since 1993 there has been indeed been a great deal of momentum in women's representation. Moreover, while only 25 of the 38 women Senators were elected rather than appointed 17 of those 25 are currently serving demonstrating that women now more than ever are fully capable of winning their offices for themselves rather than receiving at the whim of a Governor. And in every election since 1980 U.S. women have voted in higher rates than men. The question of *if* and *when* women will have equal representation in the Senate is one where's there been some disagreement and answers keep changing.

In 1987 the Feminist Majority calculated that at the then rate of progress women wouldn't achieve gender parity in either branch of Congress until 2333![69] After 1992's famous Year of the Woman, the National Organization for Women calculated that at that rate Congress would be 50-50 by 2068.

The Equal Representation in Government and Democracy () public goal is to achieve equal representation in all three branches of the federal government by as soon as 2020. Unless as some have suggested we pass legislation requiring that no state can have two Senators of the same gender to more than double the number of women in the U.S. Senate from 17 to 51 in the space of about 10 years while laudable in its ambition seems overly optimistic in a country that is currently ranked # 68 in the world for women's political leadership. (Though by all means feel free to prove us wrong!)

"Why? Because, women deserve to represented by their peers. Women deserve to have equal representation. How many women are in the House of Representatives or in the US Senate? Certainly not 50% of either house

---

69 Feminist Majority Foundation Chronology Index

is female - yet 50% or so of our population is comprised of women. Go figure. Women deserve to break that so-called glass ceiling. Shatter the s**t out of it if you will. But while trying to do this we should not oppress men just because they "oppressed" us. We should be equal, doing otherwise would simply make us hypocrites."

- Heidi Buchanan, writer

For our purposes we have chosen 2040 as a year by which we could expect women to make up fifty-one percent of the Senate which would in practice mean gaining about one woman in the Senate a year for the next thirty years. (Actually it would mean gaining 1.09th of a woman Senator every year for the next thirty years, but you can't really elect 1.09th of a person no matter how much politics may evolve so we chose to round it off.) What would having this 2040 **Senate of 51 women** *mean?*

"If men got pregnant, there would be safe, reliable methods of birth control. They'd be inexpensive too."

- Anna Quindlen, Pulitzer-winning author

"I don't believe there is one woman within the confines of this state who does not believe in birth control. I never met one. That is, I never met one who thought that she should be kept in ignorance of contraceptive methods."

- Crystal Eastman, feminist, journalist

Well for one thing it would almost assuredly mean health insurance policies wouldn't be allowed to deny coverage of birth control pills or emergency contraception while giving the heads-up to erectile dysfunction drugs. 98% of American women use birth control at some point in their lives; including 80% of Catholic women. 78% of Americans believe that for women to achieve equality they must have access to family planning services including birth control.[70] As Louise Slaughter put it, *"for most women, including women who want to have children, contraception is not an option; it is a basic health resource."* The fact that birth control and other contraceptive methods are considered politically "controversial" in America must less frequently inaccessible to lower income women is entirely the result of an unusually vocal minority

---

70 National Family Planning and Reproductive Health Association

among Conservative Christians (whose leadership is predominantly male,) that manages to exert undue influence in great part because male legislators look upon family planning and reproductive rights as some sort of special interest cultural issue that can be given lower priority.

For women legislators the issue hits a lot closer to home and while there are some prominent exceptions women politician's are a lot more likely to be adamantly pro-choice and in favor of birth control. Moreover, increased numbers of women in the Senate would profoundly change the issue in the minds of their male colleagues as well. It's hard to write something off as just a "feminist/women's" thing when 51% of your colleagues are women. A Senate with **51** women would almost assuredly **not** approve a Supreme Court justice who did not support *Roe Vs. Wade*. It's an old joke among abortion providers that even supposedly pro-life women who have been known to protest outside their clinics are known to obtain abortion services when they find themselves facing an unwanted pregnancy, (in fact one third of American women has an abortion in her lifetime) which for sheer self interest alone requires that abortion remain legal if only for oneself or one's own daughter. Debates on the Senate floor on funding Plan B contraception for instance, would be greatly enhanced by including people who might actually use it.

"If ever there were a D.C. institution in dire need of a place to plug in a breast pump, it's the Supreme Court."
    - Dahlia Lithwick, Legal Correspondent for Slate

It's also hard to imagine that with a Senate body made up with **51** women, that there would be only one woman and eight men on the Supreme Court. Supreme court justices are of course appointed rather than elected and no one would suggest that women Senators would make gender the sole determination of a nominees worthiness to the highest court in the land but those **51 women Senators** would have a very VERY hard time believing that all possible qualified candidates to the Supreme Court just happened to be male. Some of those women Senators might even personally know a few women with juris doctorates they believed were up for the job. Supreme Court Justice Ruth Bader Ginsberg said *"I would not like to be the only woman on the court."* Sadly, she was left in just that position on the retirement of Justice Sandra O

Connor; a Senate of **51** women would not allow another female justice to come to that same state of loneliness.

"If American women would increase their voting turnout by ten percent, I think we would see an end to all of the budget cuts in programs benefiting woman and children."

\- Coretta Scott King, widow of Martin Luther King Jr

This sort of Senate would no doubt pass an unprecedented amount of legislation subsidizing child care and day care centers. These Senators would not be acting under the illusion that all families have a stay at home adult to mind the kids but would be VERY aware that the vast majority of parents these days, male or female are at least partially employed outside the home and that society has to evolve with these needs. In fact there's a good chance there might even be an official daycare center started in our nation's capital not just for the children of members of Congress but for their employees as well; perhaps giant daycare centers across the Capital specializing in *all* children of federal employees. Such a policy could easily end up trickling down to the state level as well. There would not only be stronger parental leave laws on the books but also in all probability other legislation to encourage businesses to have more family friendly policies including "sick days" for employees to care for other sick relatives. It is after all women who are most likely to bear the burdens of caring for sick, infirm, or elderly family members especially among African American women.

One of the biggest handicaps in the professional world today is that women employees are often seen as less serious about their careers because they have to take time off from their duties in order to take care of family matters. This new Senate body could help lead the discussion into a new direction by arguing for the social and economic importance of the traditional care-taking work done by women that has been undervalued in the past. Anne Morrow Lindbergh <u>Gift From the Sea</u> wrote, *"By and large, mothers and housewives are the only workers who do not have regular time off. They are the great vacationless class."* With **51** women in the Senate that attitude could and would begin to change.

This would also lead to a greater political appreciation of paid caretakers as well; legislation mandating better training and higher wages for nurses, daycare workers, nursing home aides, and hospice workers would come as well. Social security benefits would also likely be more generous or at least more secure from funding cuts; an NES survey in 2004 found that women were ten points more likely to favor greater spending on social security, (68% to 58%) and were generally in favor of greater government spending overall. Women Senators would as a group be more inclined to vote for greater spending on social services be they for children, the elderly, the poor, and greater funding for American schools and would favor such spending over tax cuts. The fact that women are more likely to favor spending on social services is well known and women's greater interest in social causes is demonstrated by the fact that they make up 68% of all staff in the non-profit world. The most traditional path to the Senate usually entails a career in business or the law before becoming involved in politics but a Senate of **51** women most likely would feature a number of former of social workers, counselors, educators, and other persons from traditional "do-gooder" professions which would certainly create a cultural shift in the Senate corridors as well with Senators bringing personal experiences as high school principals or running soup kitchens to committee assignments on Education or Human services. If nothing else a Senate made up of **51** women is a Senate chamber where phrases like "bleeding heart" and "nanny state" are not likely to register with the same scorn factor as they do now.

"Women have been the guardians of life — not because we are better or purer or more innately nurturing than men, but because the men have busied themselves making war. Because of our responsibility to the next generation, because of our own love for our families and communities, it is time we women devote ourselves — wholeheartedly — to the business of making peace."

- From the Code Pink website (a women-initiated grassroots movement for world peace and social justice)

Not every government department would see its budget increase under the **51** Senate, though, there would certainly be women Senators with strong hawk leanings but as a whole women tend to favor diplomatic solutions rather than military ones to foreign policy disputes. A Senate with **51** women is not likely to approve pre-emptive military action like that in Iraq. (Wars like Afghanistan which were a direct response to an attack on a U.S. soil are a different category altogether.) The United States of America currently accounts for almost half of all military spending in the world at 45%.[71] A proportion that is greater than the next ten countries combined! Under the **51** Senate it's likely this proportion would decrease somewhat and U.S defense spending might begin to be more in line with our other industrialized allies such as the United Kingdom and China.

Other issues regarding strong arm defense tactics might well come into play too. Studies have demonstrated that women are more worried about being the victims of terrorism yet are less likely to support certain counter terrorism measures, be they torture, extralegal rendition, or even military actions.[72] An ABC news/Washington post poll conducted in 2004 found a notable gender gap on the issue of torture; 44% of men compared to 27% of women considered torture to be acceptable under some circumstances. 54% of men and only 39% of women believe that physical abuse just short of torture was sometimes acceptable and men supported the government's policies in Guantanamo Bay by 52% to 40% while women were opposed 46% to 37%. There are some competing theories as to where this gender gap on the issue of torture comes from; there's the school of thought that states that women are simply biologically hardwired to be kinder, gentler, and less enamored of violent solutions. There's the Carol Gilligan school of thought that women are socialized to see themselves as part of interdependent society and to empathize and care for others while men are socialized to be independent competitive individualists. (The whole "women are natural earth mothers and men are fierce warriors" school of thought.)

Another possibility is that women are more socialized to be aware of threats of violence, (note how most horror movies that go into "torture porn" choose young women as the preferred victims of carnage for the pleasure of their viewing audiences) and this might have the twin effects of making women more fearful of violence and yet more reluctant to use it. Whatever the reasons though, the final result is women as a group are <u>generally</u> more opposed to torture as a counter-terrorism measure than men. Now obviously this does not mean that

71 Stockholm International Peace Research Institute Yearbook 2008 Armaments, Disarmament, International Security.
72 Haider Donald and Vieux Andrea *Gender and Conditional Support for Torture in the War on Terror* <u>Politics and Gender</u> 2008 pgs 5-33

every woman senator would harshly condemn torture and practices such as rendition to overseas prison, (certainly not all the women currently serving in the U.S. Senate did) but it would have a practical effect on votes on such issues.

Let's say a piece of legislation came up allowing for the use of what it euphemistically calls "extreme interrogation methods," outside of the parameters of the U.S. judicial system or international law. Assuming that women Senators were representative of women voters at large, (and the day we achieve **51 women Senators** there is no reason to think they wouldn't be) the vote would go something like this. On this issue of "extreme interrogation" 15 women senators are in favor while 33 are opposed to the legislation. (On any vote there are always a few abstainers.) Among the male senators 25 are in support of the legislation and 20 are opposed to it. With fifty- three votes in opposition to 45 votes in favor the legislation advocating "extreme interrogation" is voted down. It doesn't matter that all the women Senators do not have the same views on the issue of torture; (in fact one of the women Senators helped co-sponsor the legislation in the first place!) merely that a solid majority of them do is enough to swing the vote. And so it goes on numerous other pieces of legislation.

"We must now fully recognize how interdependent we all have become. Only by working together, not against each other, can we have a vision of a better-managed world."
- Gro Harlem Bruntland the first woman prime minister of Norway on global sustainability.

Rachel Carson, author of *Silent Spring* is often considered to be the founder of the modern environmental movement; not coincidentally Carson was a woman. Studies show that women are up to 15% more likely than men to rate the environment a high priority, women comprise up to 2/3's of voters who cast ballots on environmental issues, women support increased funding for government environmental programs, and women are more likely than men to volunteer for and give money to environmental organizations particularly those associated with public health.[73] Women are usually the key organizers

---

73 Gould Kira, and Hosey Lance *Women Are From Earth, Men Are From Terra Firma* Grist July 31, 2007

in grassroots environmental campaigns; they are the muscle for the "green" movement. The **51** women Senate would be friendly ground for environmentalists and would sign tougher measures regarding local environmental hazards. That is a prediction based on the fact that studies show women to be less sympathetic to business on environmental concerns, more concerned with environmental issues regarding health and safety on the local level, and that women have more positive feelings about environmental activists than men do.[74] **51 women Senators** would be more likely to subsidize clean renewable energy and less generous in subsidizing oil and coal. Subsidies to nuclear energy would take a particularly harsh hit; women historically are more skeptical of nuclear power than men.[75] (So forget funding for nuclear reactors as a "solution" to peak oil.) A Senate with **51** women is more likely to demand stricter standards for clean air and clear water. They would legislate for tougher codes regarding the disposal of toxic waste. There would be more funding for the EPA to enforce its regulation codes and more funding for national parks and wilderness areas with tougher rules on proposed development projects in those areas.

"A priest can achieve great victories with an army of women at his command."

- Mary Elizabeth Braddon, Victorian Era Author

"I pray every single second of my life; not on my knees but with my work. My prayer is to lift women to equality with men. Work and worship are one with me."

- Susan B. Anthony, civil rights, women's rights leader

It's always been customary for people on Capitol Hill to boast of their religious piety but **51 women Senators** would mean there might be more genuine sincerity behind the posturing. 71% of women cite religion as very important to them but only 55% of men. Women

---

74 Caiazza, Amy and Barrett, Allison *Engaging Women in Environmental Activism; Recommendation's for Rachel's Network* Institute for Women's Policy Research IWPR Publication #1913 September, 2003

75 Solomon, Lawrence, Tomaskavic-Devey, Donald, and Risman Barbara *The gender gap and nuclear power; Attitudes in a politicized environment.*

attend church service much more frequently than men do as well; almost half of all women ages 30-49 attend church while only a third of men that age do. Women are more likely to participate in prayer or bible study groups than men and to engage in church based volunteer work as well.[76] The participants in midweek church activities are 70-80% women.[77] Christian universities now enroll almost two women for every man[78] and reform seminaries that school future rabbis are now 60% female.[79] As young people become more secular and young men especially leave their family churches in droves women are increasingly becoming the lifeblood of churches and synagogues; and those institutions that do not adapt and remain hostile to women are endangered.

Regular church goers between the ages of 21-45 are two thirds women.[80] This has implications for politics and the state as well. Generally, Republicans are somewhat more likely to attend church, but women are more likely to be members of the Democratic party, so a Senate with **51** women could signal an emergence of the Religious Left as a political force in the United States; a movement which would place a premium on the separation of church and state.[81] Moreover, the Religious Left would be gay-friendly; a Newsweek poll demonstrated that public support for gay marriage was growing among Americans and the younger you were the more likely you were to support gay

---

76 *Faith Based Funding Backed, But Church-State Doubts Abound* The Pew Research Center for People and the Press April 10, 2001

77 Barna Research Online, "Women are the Backbone of Christian Congregations in America," 6 March 2000

78 Camerin Courtney, "*O Brother, Where Art Thou?*" *Christianity Today*

79 Fishman Sylvia, and Parmer Daniel *Matrilineal Ascent/Patrilineal Descent: The Gender Imbalance in American Jewish Life* Hadassah-Brandeis Institute

80 Wuthnow Robert *"After the Baby Boomers: How Twenty- and Thirty-Somethings are Shaping the Future of American Religion"* Princeton University Press 2007

81 Nall Jeff *The Emergence of the Religious Left: An Opportunity for Religious Liberals and Humanists to Unite* The Humanist January/February 2006

marriage; and with a gender gap as well. Women were ten points more likely to support gay marriage than men 44% to 34%.[82]

"Growing up in a small Alaska town, domestic violence was that dirty little secret nobody talked about. We must start talking about it. For too long, we have been providing protection to the wrong people."

- Senator Lisa Murkowski

"When my kids were in preschool, I was part of a carpooling group. One mother sometimes showed up with bruises on her body. She always had an excuse. Then one morning, she didn't show up. Later, I learned she'd fled a violent marriage. I've always thought, If only I'd known, maybe I could have helped."

- Senator Patty Murray

1994 was the year that the Violence Against Women Act, co-sponsored by Senator Barbara Boxer and Senator Joe Biden, was passed with six women in the U.S. Senate. It's fair to say that with **51** women in the U.S. Senate the impact on legislation regarding such matters as domestic violence and sexual assault would be enormous. Currently one of the leading causes of death among pregnant women in the United States is homicide; (31% of all injury related deaths among pregnant women,) and most of the time they are murdered by their intimate partners.[83] In 2008 the National Crime Victimization Survey conducted by the U.S. Department of Justice reported that nearly 250,000 persons were raped or sexually assaulted in 2007, (women are ten times more likely than men to report being the victims of sexual assault) and over half a million crimes of violence perpetrated against women by their intimate partners-an 42% increase in the number of such crimes committed in 2005. (By comparison the number of incidents of men who were violently assaulted by intimate partners went down; indeed except for simple assault which went up 3% all other crimes surveyed that year decreased; except for rape and domestic violence.) Representative Mark Green of Wisconsin said, *"If the numbers we see in domestic violence were applied to terrorism or gang violence, the entire country would be up in arms, and it would be the lead story on the*

---

82 Campo Flores Arian *A Gay Marriage Surge* <u>Newsweek Web Exclusive</u> December 5, 2008

83 <u>The American Journal of Public Health</u> 2005

news every night" In order to understand how the presence of women in the U.S. Senate would help this situation consider the following examples:

- Representative Carolyn Maloney (NY)who had an attorney friend who was battered by her minister husband authored and helped secure a law providing federal funding to clear the backlogs of rape kits that had been collected but never entered into law enforcement DNA databases. The Rape Abuse and National Incest network called it *"the most important anti-rape legislation ever considered by Congress."*[84]

- Secretary of Labor Hilda Solis has a niece who survived sexual assault and a sister who survived domestic violence; when serving in the California state Senate authored 17 bills to prevent domestic violence that became laws![85]

- Senator Patty Murray of the state of Washington in 2005 introduced the SAFE Act to overcome certain economic obstacles that keep victims of domestic violence trapped in abusive relationships. Again there was a personal component to this; years before she became a Senator when her children were in pre-school Patty Murray carpooled with another young mother who kept appearing with bruises. One day this woman didn't show up and Murray later learned she had been fleeing an abusive husband. Murray would later recount, *"I've always thought, 'if only I'd known, maybe I could have helped.'"*

We are not going to say that **51 women Senators** would guarantee better justice for the victims of rape and domestic violence, but it would certainly create more pressure from above to investigate the causes behind these crimes and to change the culture of the courts to better serve the needs of victims. The Family Violence Prevention and Services Act was budgeted $125 million in 2008 despite assessments

---

84 *Fighting Sexual Violence with DNA"*, <u>Rape Abuse and Incest National Network</u>
85 *The New Team: Hilda L. Solis* <u>The New York Times</u> February 26, 2009

that they needed $175 million.[86] By way of comparison $169 million was budgeted to build new prisons and $2.8 billion to stop the spread of illegal drugs.[87] Imagine what would happen if the Federal government put as much resources into preventing sexual assault and domestic violence that it does to prosecuting people for growing marijuana?!?

> *"The connection between women's human rights, gender equality, socioeconomic development and peace is increasingly apparent."*
> - Mahnaz Afkhami, Iranian American human rights activist

> *"Gender equality is critical to the development and peace of every nation."*
> - Kofi Annan, Secretary General to the UN

It would not just be women in the United States whose lives would benefit from the **51** Senate. The proposed International Violence Against Women Act of 2007, that failed to receive a majority vote in either the House or Senate would almost assuredly pass in the **51** Senate of the future. The provisions of this legislation which include increased legal and judicial protection to address violence against women and girls, increases in health sector capacity to protect women and girls from violence that would be integrated into pre-existing programs focusing on child survival, women's health and HIV/AIDS programs to change community norms on the subject of violence towards women and young girls, improving women's access to education and economic opportunities, and training of overseas foreign security forces on violence against women. Currently there is an ongoing battle in the Senate over approval of the CEDAW (Convention on the Elimination of All Forms of Discrimination Against Women) treaty; a treaty that was first adopted in 1979 and of the 192 UN Members the United States is one of only eight nations not to ratify it. (Our fellow holdouts being Sudan, Somalia, Qatar, Iran, Nauru, Palau, and Tonga. We're among great company on this one!) It's hard to believe that a Senate with **51** women would fail to CEDAW and join other global organizations that fight for women's political rights abroad. This has immense implications beyond the status of women. Studies of HIV in Latin America and Africa showed that the better educated women

---

86 *FY 2008 Appropriations* National Coalition Against Domestic Violence
87 Office of Management and Budget Department of Justice

were the lower their risks for HIV infection.[88] This shows that battling the AIDS pandemic is as much about empowering women to demand the use of condoms as it is providing them with condoms in the first place.

Ken Hackett of Catholic Relief Services when explaining his organization's focus of empowering women as the linchpin of their campaign against global poverty wrote, *"Women are often the poorest members of a community and control the fewest resources. But with more assets, they often do the most to impact their families and communities for the better."* Muhammad Yunus, Nobel prize winner, and founder of the Grameen bank microfinance program in Bangladesh explained one reason his organization concentrated on making loans to poor women was because they were more likely to spend additional resources on their children and household than male borrowers were. For U.S. aid initiatives abroad to be truly effective they have to focus more on the culture and politics of gender in the countries they serve; and having women legislators voting on those initiatives is certainly one way to accomplish that.

On the horizon in 2010 there are 36 Senate elections. 6 of the current women Senators' terms will expire then: Barbara Boxer, Barbara Mikulski, Blanche Lincoln, Lisa Murkowski, Patty Murray, and Kristen Gillibrand. Gillibrand was appointed to replace Senator Hillary Clinton after Hillary's move to be Secretary of State, so she will be running for election for the first time. Murkowski, Lincoln, and Boxer have plans to run for re-election. Mikulski and Murray have not made announcements to run as yet.

At 70 years of age Senator Boxer will be seeking her 4th Senate term, where as Senator Mikulski, **if** she should decide to run, would be seeking her 5th term at age 73.

In Ohio, Republican Senator George Voinovich is retiring and there will be contenders from both parties hoping to be his replacement. At least one woman has declared her candidacy, Democrat Jennifer Brunner who is Ohio's current Secretary of State. There is also a possibility that Ohio Congresswoman Marcy Kaptur may run for the Senate after 27 years in the House.

---

88 Grown Caren, Gupta Rao Geeta, Pande Rahini *Taking action to improve women's health through gender equality and women's empowerment.* Lancet #365 2005, pgs 541-543

Similarly in Missouri the current Democratic Secretary of State, Robin Carnahan, has announced that she will be seeking the U.S. Senate seat that will become vacant in 2010 by the retirement of Missouri's current Republican Senator Kit Bond. Robin is the daughter of the late Mel Carnahan who was Governor of Missouri, and Senator Jean Carnahan whose story was told in a previous chapter.

Florida Republican Senator Mel Martinez is another who has already announced his retirement in 2010 and there are at least 4 women who have expressed interest in running for his slot.

3 other male Senators have announced that they would be retiring and not running for re-election in 2010: Republican Sam Brownback of Kansas, Republican Judd Gregg from New Hampshire, and Democrat Ted Kaufman from Delaware (appointed to fill Joe Biden's seat when Biden was elected VP). Perhaps some women candidates will step up in those states.

Republican Governor of Hawaii Laura Lingle could challenge 8 term Democratic Senator Daniel Inouye, who at 86 years of age has decided to seek re-election. Both of these Hawaii politicians are very popular.

Democratic Congresswoman Jan Schakowsky who represents Illinois' 9th District may run for the U.S. Senate slot that Senator Roland Burris now holds. Burris was appointed with considerable controversy by impeached Illinois Governor Rod Blagojevich to fill the Senate seat left vacant by Barack Obama when he became President.

Democratic Senate Majority Leader Harry Reid of Nevada will seek a 5th term in 2010 at age 71. There are rumors that he may be challenged by a 2 women, one from each party.

There are possibilities of 2 Democratic Congresswomen Carolyn Maloney (14th District) and Carolyn McCarthy (4th District) making a challenge against New York Senator Kristen Gillibrand.

There are 10 of the other states where more women may contend and perhaps add to the number of women in the Senate. 2010 will be a interesting year to see how many female incumbents retain their seats, how many retire, and how many new women reach the position of U.S. Senator. It will be difficult for women to gain seats over the existing number of 17 if several incumbents retire.

Prognosticating is a tricky business and perhaps we're wrong to expect that **51 women Senators** would have such dramatic results, but still it seems a worthy experiment to attempt. Golda Meir put it best when she said, "*Whether women are better than men I cannot say - but they are certainly no worse.*"

51 ?

CONCLUSION

"If you want something said ask a man....if you want something done ask a woman."

> \- Margaret Thatcher, Prime Minister of Great Britain

"I think it's about time we voted for senators with breasts. After all we've been voting for boobs long enough."

> \- Claire Sargent Senatorial Candidate for Arizona

"Somewhere out in this audience may even be someone who will one day follow in my footsteps, and preside over the White House as the President's spouse. I wish him well!"

> \- First Lady Barbara Bush at Wellesley College

The old comedic line for why women should have more political power is that they could not possibly screw things up more than men already have. (Given the current state of the economy and the war there seems to be a bit of gallows humor to that joke these days.) We've already stated how we think a Senate with fifty-one women might vote differently and why that could be good for America, but voting differences aside, the biggest reason we want a Senate with **51** women is because of these three little words...."We the People." Those three words are America's great promise; a democracy by the people for the people...and the word "people" doesn't mean just men. (Though, the founding fathers only gave white land owning men voting rights.)

Ultimately, we need **51** women in the Senate because women are 51% of the American people and that is that. And we do not expect them to be all white women either but black women, women of Hispanic or Latino origin, Asian women, women who do not identify themselves as straight either and that same amount of diversity would be present in men as well.

In 1907, swimmer Annette Kellerman of Australia was arrested while on tour in the United States of America for "indecent exposure,".... her swimsuit revealed arms, legs, and her neck. That same swimsuit to modern swimmers would seem hopelessly antiquated and constrained; a curiosity of a long bygone era. We actually hope this book will someday be the same way; "Imagine," we expect to hear people a century from now, "they wrote books about if it was even possible for women to be 51% of the U.S. Senate...what was the matter with those people?"

As advanced and modern and progressive as we think we are as a country, there are still 27 of our 50 states that have never elected a woman to the Senate so there is still much room for more of those "firsts" we've been talking about for years to come. But for the sake of women's equality we should hope that eventually the day will arrive when it will no longer be historical record-breaking news that a woman was "the first woman" to hold any office in any state or district.

Shirley Chisholm once noted that it was on some level profoundly disappointing that she had a claim to fame by being the first African American woman in Congress; it was a testament to the fact that American society was neither just nor free. Writing this book is something of a similar experience; yet there was another way to look at Chisholm's victory. It showed that things were (however, slowly,) beginning to change; forty-four years after Shirley Chisholm was elected to Congress and thirty-six years after she ran for President, Senator Barack Obama was elected as President of the United States. It's discoursing to think that over three hundred years after the Senate was formed equal representation in it is still a matter of hypothesis but it's encouraging to see how much stronger that hypothesis is than even fifteen years ago.

We close with these words by Susan B. Anthony:

"There will never be complete equality until women themselves help to make laws and elect lawmakers."

Over a hundred and fifty years later, Susan, we're still trying.

Resources

Feminist Majority Foundation Online
The White House Project
The National Organization for Women
Emily's List
Code Pink
Center for AmWomen & Politics
Am Association of University Women
Running Start

www.51womensenators.com

About the authors

Winnie Frolik…was born and raised in Pittsburgh, Pennsylvania, the child of two lawyers. She received her Bachelor of Arts in Creative Writing and English Literature (double major) from the University of Pittsburgh. She has been diagnosed with Asperger's Syndrome otherwise known as high functioning autism.

After becoming depressed by the 2004 presidential election she decided to do something constructive and began working in the non-profit sector. She did a stint in Americorps Conservation Corps working in state parks in New Hampshire, an internship with the Pittsburgh AIDS Task Force, before coming to Washington D.C. and joining Project Change another Americorps program.

Then she worked for one year with Youth and Family Service of the Greater Washington DC YMCA which provides mentoring, after-school programs, summer camps, parenting classes, and intervention for underprivileged youth and families.

Winnie also served as the Grants/Development Assistant for the Jewish Foundation for Group Homes which runs a number of assisted living group homes for disabled adults; from the mentally ill, to autistics, to people with Down Syndrome, to Hearing and or Visual impairment. She is currently enrolled at the Art Institute of Washington studying baking and pastry and working on another book project.

Billy HerZIG…is from Ft. Worth, Texas. During his 25 plus years as a music producer, engineer, writer Zig has produced over 50 independent CD projects, worked with many well-known songwriters and artists, and performed for 1000s of people as a musician. Some of his productions and compositions have been heard all over the world on radio, TV, movies and advertisements.

Zig spent 9 years as a staff writer for various music publishers in Nashville including Sony, Warner/Chappell, and Music Daily. He is the writer of the #1 country hit "Right From the Start" recorded by Earl Thomas Conley (RCA 1989), which was also used in the movie *Roadhouse*.

Through the years Zig has recorded and produced over 1000 demos for various writers and for all the major publishers and record labels in Nashville. He has also helped guide the direction of many young songwriters, musicians, and singers.

He has been a fan, follower and student of many of the women Senators, Representatives, and Governors since the early 1990's beginning with Ann Richards (former Governor of Texas) and the humor of Molly Ivans.

Zig records and produces music in Nashville, Tennessee and Arlington, Texas and is currently working on several books and documentaries (NOT about politics).

www.ingramcontent.com/pod-product-compliance
Lightning Source LLC
Chambersburg PA
CBHW061304280526
45784CB00002B/891